U.S. Department of Justice
Office of Justice Programs
Office for Victims of Crime

D1466927

Transforming Victim Services

FINAL REPORT

Innovation • Partnerships
Safer Neighborhoods

JUSTICE FOR VICTIMS
JUSTICE FOR ALL

Office for Victims of Crime
OVC

U.S. Department of Justice
Office of Justice Programs
810 Seventh Street NW.
Washington, DC 20531

Eric H. Holder, Jr.
Attorney General

Mary Lou Leary
Acting Assistant Attorney General

Joye E. Frost
Acting Director, Office for Victims of Crime

Office of Justice Programs
Innovation • Partnerships • Safer Neighborhoods
www.ojp.usdoj.gov

Office for Victims of Crime
www.ovc.gov

NCJ 239957

May 2013

The mission of the Office for Victims of Crime is to enhance the Nation's capacity to assist crime victims and to provide leadership in changing attitudes, policies, and practices to promote justice and healing for all victims of crime.

The Office of Justice Programs (OJP) provides federal leadership in developing the Nation's capacity to prevent and control crime, administer justice, and assist victims. OJP has six components: the Bureau of Justice Assistance; the Bureau of Justice Statistics; the National Institute of Justice; the Office of Juvenile Justice and Delinquency Prevention; the Office for Victims of Crime; and the Office of Sex Offender Sentencing, Monitoring, Apprehending, Registering, and Tracking. More information about OJP can be found at www.ojp.gov.

U.S. Department of Justice
Office of Justice Programs
810 Seventh Street NW.
Washington, DC 20531

Eric H. Holder, Jr.
Attorney General

Mary Lou Leary
Acting Assistant Attorney General

Joye E. Frost
Acting Director, Office for Victims of Crime

Office of Justice Programs
Innovation • Partnerships • Safer Neighborhoods
www.ojp.usdoj.gov

Office for Victims of Crime
www.ovc.gov

NCJ 239957

May 2013

The mission of the Office for Victims of Crime is to enhance the Nation's capacity to assist crime victims and to provide leadership in changing attitudes, policies, and practices to promote justice and healing for all victims of crime.

The Office of Justice Programs (OJP) provides federal leadership in developing the Nation's capacity to prevent and control crime, administer justice, and assist victims. OJP has six components: the Bureau of Justice Assistance; the Bureau of Justice Statistics; the National Institute of Justice; the Office of Juvenile Justice and Delinquency Prevention; the Office for Victims of Crime; and the Office of Sex Offender Sentencing, Monitoring, Apprehending, Registering, and Tracking. More information about OJP can be found at www.ojp.gov.

Transforming Victim Services

JUSTICE FOR VICTIMS
JUSTICE FOR ALL

Office for Victims of Crime

OVC

Contents

Executive Summary

The goal for Vision 21: Transforming Victim Services (Vision 21) is simple yet profound: to permanently alter the way we treat victims of crime in America. The Office for Victims of Crime (OVC) at the Office of Justice Programs, U.S. Department of Justice, and many others who work in the victim assistance field recognize the need for a better way to respond to crime victims. We seek a comprehensive and systemic approach, drawing from a wide range of tangible yet difficult to access resources, including legislation, more flexible funding, research, and practice, to change how we meet victims' needs and how we address those who perpetrate crime. We have heard the call for a better way, and it is our fervent hope that Vision 21 creates that path.

Vision 21 grew from a series of meetings sponsored by OVC across the country, to facilitate conversations about the victim assistance field. These meetings brought together crime victim advocates and allied professionals to exchange information and ideas about enduring and emerging issues and how we treat victims of crime. What emerged from those intense and fruitful discussions was a common understanding about current challenges facing victims and, most importantly, a shared expression of the urgent need for change. Vision 21 is the result of those conversations. We believe it can be our call to action—the motivation to address the needs of crime victims in a radically different way.

Our discussions and research centered on four topics: (1) defining the role of the victim assistance field in the overall response to crime and delinquency in the United States; (2) building the field's capacity to better serve victims; (3) addressing enduring issues in the field; and (4) identifying emerging issues in the field. It was an ambitious agenda for a relatively brief timeframe, but one that was long overdue.

History

Vision 21 began with the perspective that the crime victims' movement is still a fledgling field—

a phenomenon of the past 40 years. The movement crystallized at the national level in 1981 with the proclamation of the first National Crime Victims' Rights Week to honor courageous victims and their surviving family members. The release of a groundbreaking report a year later—*The Final Report of the President's Task Force on Victims of Crime*—led to the passage of the Victims of Crime Act (VOCA) of 1984. This landmark legislation established the Crime Victims Fund to provide stable funding for victim assistance programs and to change the landscape of a criminal justice system that was unwelcoming and all too often hostile to victims' interests.

The next major examination came in 1998, with OVC's release of *New Directions from the Field: Victims' Rights and Services for the 21st Century*, noting substantial progress made since 1981 with recommendations for improving victims' rights, services, and freedom from discrimination. By 2010, OVC leadership recognized it was time for the field to revisit those goals, assess the progress made toward reaching them, and chart a course for the future. At the same time, an outpouring of concern from victim advocacy groups and their allies illuminated a growing number of victims being turned away for lack of funding or the ability to provide appropriate services. The advocates detailed the additional challenges in reaching and serving victims of emergent crimes such as human trafficking, child commercial sexual exploitation, and financial fraud. Clearly, the time is here for a renewed assessment of the state of victims' services, which can only come from those who know it best—crime victims, victim service providers, and advocates.

The Vision 21 strategic initiative, launched by OVC in fall 2010, competitively awarded funding to five organizations: the National Crime Victim Law Institute, the National Center for Victims of Crime (NCVC), the Vera Institute of Justice Center on Victimization and Safety, OVC's Training and Technical Assistance Center, and the National Crime Victims Research and Treatment Center of the Medical University of South Carolina. For 18 months, the partners examined the status of the victim assistance field and explored both new and perennial challenges. Five stakeholder forums were held, with representatives of traditional and non-traditional victim service providers, from NCVC to a community rape crisis center, from sexual assault nurse examiners to prosecutors. They discussed the problems they saw in the field and recommended ways to advance the state of victim assistance in the United States. OVC and its partners also conducted a review of relevant literature, hosted interactive discussions at conferences and meetings with state VOCA administrators and other key constituencies and, through OVC's Web site, invited interested parties to join the discussion.

This final report reflects those discussions. As such, it is a document created by the field, for the field. We at OVC hope that crime victim service providers and advocates embrace Vision 21 as their own. OVC and its partner organizations believe that it unites voices from the field, including crime victims and those who speak on behalf of victims who are not able to speak for themselves. The success of this vision lies with the field and its desire to overcome challenges—for only the field can drive transformational change.

Challenges

All who took part in Vision 21 quickly identified a great need to expand the base of knowledge about crime victimization. This report examines the need for victim-related statistical data, evidence-based practices, and program evaluation. Although Vision 21 identifies some exemplary applications of current research, there is no comprehensive body of empirical data to guide policymakers, funders, and practitioners. We know that research is the road, not the roadblock, to victim-centered practice and policy.

Equally troubling was the absence of certain victims' voices and perspectives in criminal justice policy debates, which remain focused primarily on the prosecution and incarceration of offenders. OVC and stakeholders in the field, on the other hand, routinely heard from individuals who shared a

different vision of justice. For those victimized by family members rather than strangers, as well as victims from Indian Country and crime-ridden city neighborhoods, justice is not always about a retributive system. These victims brought to the conversation a passion for promoting broader policies of prevention and innovative public safety programs to hold offenders accountable and reduce recidivism while promoting healing for victims.

Another of the report's findings affirms the increasing difficulty of defining the victim assistance field. We grappled with the question of whether or not "victim assistance" includes allied practitioners—that is, professionals who do not self-identify as victim service providers, such as emergency room physicians, prosecutors, and court personnel. We agreed that we must cast a wide net to connect with the mental health, indigent defense, juvenile justice, and other fields that intersect with victim assistance. We discussed the historically low salaries for victim service providers who perform some of society's toughest jobs. We also acknowledged the inherent conflict between a focus on responding to a specialized type of victimization and the need to expand that focus—beyond the presenting victimization—to the holistic needs of the victim.

Report findings reflect the sobering reality that although some violent crime rates may be decreasing, the incidence of other types of victimization in this country—including crime perpetrated in cyberspace, human trafficking, and crime committed against older people and those with disabilities—may not even be captured by traditional survey instruments or reported to law enforcement. A staggering 42 percent of victims never report serious violent crime to law enforcement.[1] We need to know why. Stakeholders described a maze of overlapping, complex legal issues facing victims; for example, a single victimization can involve immigration status, civil legal assistance, administrative law remedies, and rights enforcement.

The use of technology was woven through the Vision 21 discussions as well. Although it can drive new types of crime such as online child pornography and can facilitate other crimes such as stalking, technology can be a powerful tool in expanding

---

[1] *Victimizations Not Reported to the Police,* 2006–2010, National Crime Victimization Survey: Special Report, August 2012, http://bjs.ojp.usdoj.gov/content/pub/pdf/vnrp0610.pdf (accessed October 23, 2012).

victims' access to services. Web-based and mobile technology offer amazing potential for outreach and collaboration and increasingly can be used to bring services directly to victims. There are challenges: technology is not cheap, we must address privacy and confidentiality concerns, and too many organizations that already struggle with funding do not have the money to invest in technology. However, technology is critical to building the infrastructure for the systematic collection and analysis of victimization data and evaluation of programs. It also offers a potential solution to the increasing burden placed on providers by administrative and financial reporting requirements.

Overcoming these barriers, including the research gap, lack of a technology infrastructure, obstacles to collaboration, and insufficient funding, means taking a hard look at the statutory framework for the funding and administration of much of the victim assistance at the state and local levels—VOCA. VOCA is permanently authorized but has been amended infrequently since its passage. It remains rooted in the practices of the early 1980s: direct services focused on crisis response provided through a substantially volunteer workforce. VOCA is largely silent on the issues of prevention, research, and program evaluation; the use of technology; the need for collaborative and multi-jurisdictional responses to victims; and the capacity of organizations to provide increasingly complex and longer-term support to victims. Raising the cap on Crime Victims Fund spending as proposed in the President's 2014 Budget provides additional resources to begin to drive transformative change in the victim assistance field.

These challenges offer an unprecedented opportunity to craft a new vision for the future. Against this background, we present our vision for transforming victim services in the 21st century.

Vision 21 Beacons

Appearing throughout the report are boxes containing "Vision 21 Beacons." Each Beacon provides examples of innovative programs and practices in the topic area of the chapter in which it appears that may help to "light the way" into the future framed by Vision 21.

Recommendations

The discussions that formed the basis for Vision 21 demonstrated that only a truly comprehensive and far-reaching approach would achieve the vast changes needed to move the field forward. Stakeholders saw that a holistic approach to victims' needs is essential but will require unprecedented collaboration among service providers, an ongoing challenge for the field.

Vision 21's reach must extend to mental health, medical, indigent defense, research, homeless advocacy, juvenile justice, legal services, and other fields that play an integral role in promoting safe and healthy communities. Substantial, systematic, and sustained collaboration will be essential to fulfilling the promise of Vision 21. The final chapter of this report outlines Vision 21 stakeholders' recommendations for beginning the transformative change, which fall into the following four broad categories:

1. **Conduct continuous rather than episodic strategic planning** in the victim assistance field to effect real change in research, policy, programming, and capacity building.

2. **Support the development of research** to build a body of evidence-based knowledge and generate, collect, and analyze quantitative and qualitative data on victimization, emerging victimization trends, services and behaviors, and enforcement efforts.

3. **Ensure the statutory, policy, and programmatic flexibility to address enduring and emerging crime victim issues.**

4. **Build and institutionalize capacity through an infusion of technology, training, and innovation to ensure that the field is equipped to meet the demands of the 21st century.**

When OVC and its project partners first embarked on the Vision 21 process, we hesitated to use "Transforming Victim Services" as part of the Vision 21 title. We wondered if advocates and service providers in the field would interpret "transforming" as dismissive of the current state of practice or minimizing the extraordinary successes of the pioneering advocates in the field. Yet, we found that Vision 21 clarified that practitioners in this field, which began as a transformative movement, would not be content with maintaining the status quo or a less than bold exploration of the issues.

Now, 30 years after the release of the 1982 *Final Report of the President's Task Force on Victims of Crime,* we believe that the *Vision 21: Transforming Victim Services Final Report* captures another seminal opportunity in the history of the crime victims' movement. Armed with the information summarized in this report, we must take the next step: turning today's vision into tomorrow's reality for crime victims in this country.

CHAPTER 1
Forging a Future Informed by Research

Vision 21 Statement

Victims of crime will be served through a national commitment to support robust, ongoing research and program evaluation that informs the quality and practice of victim services throughout the Nation. Evidence-based, research-informed victim service programs will become the standard of excellence in providing assistance and support to victims of all types of crime.

Making Research a 21st Century Priority

The Vision 21 initiative engaged a broad group of stakeholders in a discussion about the strategic and philosophical challenges and opportunities they face in serving crime victims. The Office for Victims of Crime (OVC) interviewed victims, providers of direct services, and other practitioners who play an essential role in supporting victims, including those in law enforcement, the court system, medical and mental health care, social services, academia, technology and telecommunications, and federal, tribal, state, and local governments. The stakeholders' most singular finding was the dearth of data and research in the field. That gap is reflected in every other finding of the Vision 21 initiative as well, so it is fitting that this report begins by focusing on the role of research in victim services policy and practice.

Vision 21 participants overwhelmingly expressed an urgent need to expand the knowledge base about crime victimization and effective response. They viewed research, development of evidence-based practices, and program evaluation as the foundation of successful victim services policy and practice. As the victim services field competes for scarce resources, it must have the knowledge and tools to document the value and cost effectiveness of its services. Vision 21's highest priority is promoting evidence-based strategies and programs that

will expand the profession's fundamental understanding of who is affected by crime, how they are affected, what works to help victims recover from their trauma, and what other issues affect the delivery of services to victims and the protection of their legal rights.

This chapter summarizes (1) the current state of victim-related research and its accessibility; (2) the interdependence of basic research, evidence-based practices, and program evaluation; and (3) major challenges to the integration of research in victim services.

The Three Research Pillars

Vision 21 participants agree that three research pillars must play a significantly greater role in shaping victim services in the 21st century:

1. **Basic Research.** Crime victim services must be designed with a clear understanding of who is victimized and by whom, what victims need, why some victims access services and others do not, and to what extent victims' rights are enforced.

2. **Program Evaluation.** Providers of crime victim services must make ongoing evaluation an integral part of their programming to ensure continual quality control and improvement in support of victim safety and well-being. They must continually assess the effectiveness of practices now in use and new practices as they are developed.

3. **Evidence-Based Practices.** Crime victim service providers should expand their use of practices that have been proved to be effective and reliable for the broad array of victims they serve.

Research Pillar 1: Basic Research

Serving crime victims requires a solid foundation of research about the causes and consequences of crime and its impact on victims. Unfortunately, for too many years victim service providers have lacked empirical data to guide their program development and implementation. We need research to give us better answers to basic questions about victimization: Who is victimized, by what crimes, and by whom? Who does or does not seek services, and why? Which victims report the crime to law enforcement, which do not, and why? How reliably are victims' legal rights enforced across the Nation?

The first places to look for answers are the two major national crime data research programs that measure the magnitude, nature, and, to a more limited degree, the impact of crime in the United States. The U.S. Department of Justice (DOJ) administers both of these programs: the Federal Bureau of Investigation's (FBI) Uniform Crime Reports (UCR) and the Bureau of Justice Statistics' (BJS) National Crime Victimization Survey (NCVS).[2]

UCR is an annual compilation of offense and arrest data reported voluntarily by more than 17,000 local police departments nationwide. UCR data reflect only the most serious offenses associated with each criminal incident, including rape, robbery, aggravated assault, burglary, larceny, theft, motor vehicle theft, and arson. Simple assault is measured only when an arrest is made. Except in its Supplementary Homicide Report, UCR does not measure the impact of crime on victims.

NCVS is a telephone and in-person survey of a nationally representative sample of persons age 12 or older. It provides data on personal crime victimization, including rape and sexual assault, robbery, aggravated or simple assault, and larceny and property crime, including burglary, motor vehicle, and other types of theft. NCVS encompasses data on crimes reported and not reported to the police, as well as limited data on the type of assistance provided by law enforcement (when crimes are reported) and whether the victim received services from a victim service agency. Separate NCVS supplements also provide statistics on stalking, identity theft, school crime, and contacts between the police and the public.

Despite the breadth of NCVS and UCR data, because of the limitations of these two surveys (described in the Appendix), there are significant gaps in our understanding of the prevalence and impact of many forms of criminal victimization. Compounding this dearth of information is the fact that over the past decade, the nature and reach of crime—and its implications for victims—have changed dramatically. For example—

- U.S. demographics have changed substantially as the result of immigration, changing birthrates, and longer life expectancy, resulting in greater diversity among victim populations.

- Remarkable advances in technology and telecommunications have created a breeding ground for new crimes, the perpetration of traditional crimes in new ways, the ability to victimize many people through a single criminal enterprise, and the capacity to victimize individuals across national borders.

- Seismic attitudinal shifts in American culture have made populations of previously underserved victims more visible, such as minor victims of domestic sex trafficking; victims with disabilities; lesbian, gay, bisexual, transgender, and queer or questioning (LGBTQ) victims; and older victims of sexual abuse.

vision 21 BEACON

Standardized, automated data collection. Pennsylvania instituted a Data Collection, Reporting, and Outcomes Project to provide victim service programs with a standardized data collection and reporting system. All VOCA grantees, as well as grantees funded through the state sexual assault or domestic violence coalitions, are required to use the aggregate reporting and outcome reporting parts of the system, with the option of using the client data management aspects of the system as well. Funders can now generate data reports without having to burden local providers.

---

[2] For more detail about the methodology of the UCR and NCVS, see the Appendix.

- Increased globalization has magnified the impact of crime that may originate in other countries, such as human trafficking and crimes committed against American citizens in foreign countries or on cruise ships in international waters.

These and other major changes in society are transforming the nature of crime victimization. The victim services field must respond with programs and practices informed by up-to-date, accurate data that are adequate to meet the needs of the expanding population of crime victims.

More information is needed, for example, about the incidence and prevalence of crime victimization in historically underserved populations, as well as the barriers they face in asserting their rights as victims and gaining access to services. These populations include persons with disabilities, boys and young men of color, adults and juveniles in detention settings, youth and women who are trafficked, LGBTQ victims, undocumented immigrants, Americans who are victimized while living in foreign countries, and American Indian/Alaska Native peoples. Logistical, cultural, and practical hurdles to studying and reaching underserved groups must not deter the field's resolve to provide culturally competent, appropriate services to all victims of crime.

The field also must become more knowledgeable about the reach and impact of crimes new to the victim services landscape, such as **cybercrime** in its many permutations: online identity theft, financial fraud, hacking, cyber-stalking, online child pornography and sexual exploitation, and information piracy and forgery. New kinds of online victimization are expanding dramatically as technology continues to spawn new tools of use to criminals.

Once hidden in the shadows, **human trafficking** is becoming more and more visible in cities, towns, and rural areas. We need data about the origins and immigration status of trafficking victims and perpetrators, as well as the factors that contribute to the sex trafficking of children in the United States and the interventions that are most effective in rescuing them. We need to know what percentage

of victims participate in the criminal investigations that are essential to bringing traffickers to justice, and the reasons they are willing and able to take part in these investigations.

Responding to victims harmed by **environmental crime** is beyond the current reach and capacity of most in the victim services field, due largely to a pervasive lack of data about victims and the defining characteristics of such crimes, as well as the long-term unfolding of evidence about the criminal nature of some environmental "accidents." Nevertheless, Vision 21 stakeholders stressed the importance of serving these victims and holding corporate and other offenders accountable for the harm they cause to victims. Regardless of whether nature, human error, or criminal acts cause the damage, environmental incidents may impact crime victims. After the 2010 Deepwater Horizon oil spill in the Gulf of Mexico, for example, the Louisiana Coalition Against Domestic Violence reported large spikes in reports to the state domestic violence hotline, accompanied by a dramatic drop in private funding to support domestic violence programs.

Finally, critical questions persist regarding many **enduring challenges** such as effective interventions for victims of domestic violence, sexual violence, and child abuse. American society has yet to embrace the causal relationship between childhood victimization and later criminal behavior or repeat victimization. Nor do we clearly understand the full range and impact of property crime (burglary, motor vehicle theft, robbery, and arson). We also have little information about violent crime committed against Americans who reside in or travel to foreign countries.

Addressing these and other gaps in the knowledge base will require the **expansion of NCVS.** To initiate the process, OVC provided BJS with funding to expand the data collection activities of NCVS[3] to extend beyond simply enumerating the number of crimes to collecting more descriptive information about victims, the services they receive, and their reasons for accessing those services. The research will help identify the service gaps that have been shared anecdotally by the field for years but which

---

[3] Remarks by Mary Lou Leary, Acting Assistant Attorney General, Office of Justice Programs, U.S. Department of Justice, at the National Crime Victims' Rights Week Awards Ceremony, April 20, 2012, www.ojp.usdoj.gov/newsroom/speeches/2012/12_0420mlleary.pdf (accessed May 11, 2012).

have never been documented empirically. We must also expand the FBI's National Incident-Based Reporting System (NIBRS) to compile **a nationally representative system of police administrative records** that provides detailed descriptions of crimes, victims, and police responses to victimization. This information will lead to a greater understanding of very specific types of victimization and subgroups of victims that are not well captured by victim surveys. It also will help us compare victims known to the police with those served by victim service agencies, so we can more readily identify underserved groups.

Research Pillar 2: Program Evaluation

The second research pillar for the victim services field is program evaluation—systematic, objective processes for determining the impact of a policy, program, or practice. Using a variety of research designs and methodologies (logic models, service observations, client surveys, cost-benefit analyses, and others), program evaluation answers questions about whether and to what extent a program is achieving its strategic goals and objectives. When conducted properly, program evaluation provides information to help managers make informed decisions about future program enhancements and modifications.

Victim service programs throughout the United States increasingly perform ongoing program evaluation, due in part to a growing demand for accountability by government, foundation, and other funding sources.[4] Not surprising for a field comprising mostly non-researchers, however, program evaluations by these agencies vary greatly in quality and content. Most evaluations include a wide range of process measures, which focus on program implementation (e.g., number of victims served, number of referrals made, number of cases closed, types of services offered) and outcome measures, which focus on a program's effectiveness (e.g., change in program usage, change in satisfaction with case outcomes, reduction in recurring victimization, change in reporting future incidents to police).[5] Field leadership should have a fluent command of a wide range of program evaluation measures to examine the social, financial, and organizational effectiveness of their programs.[6]

Vision 21 stakeholders anticipate that evaluation-appropriate data collection on program performance will become routine and fully automated via technology in the 21st century. Program evaluation will tell us if the needs of crime victims are being met, whether various approaches are cost-effective, and how programs can be improved to better serve crime victims, their families, and communities.

vision 21 BEACON

Outcome measures. Georgia's Criminal Justice Coordinating Council worked with VOCA and Violence Against Women Act sub-grantees to develop a set of outcome measures. Advisory groups representing each major program type developed performance measures best suited for that type of program. Agencies are encouraged to go beyond the required core set of outcomes they measure to best fit their service system and clients. Through an online reporting system and the use of standardized core performance measures, including output, satisfaction, and outcome measures, victim service agencies in Georgia will be able to fully integrate program evaluation with program implementation activities while maintaining a level of transparency and accountability with funders that was previously unattainable. The Criminal Justice Coordinating Council began receiving data in May 2013.

---

[4] Mandi Larsen, Corey Tax, and Shelly Botuck, "Standardizing Practice at a Victim Services Organization: A Case Analysis Illustrating the Role of Evaluation," *Administration in Social Work* 33: 439–449, 2009.

[5] For a longer list of process and outcome measures, see www.bja.gov/evaluation/program-law-enforcement/vsp2.htm (accessed May 12, 2012).

[6] Some OJP agencies offer training to help practitioners increase their capacity to conduct evaluations. OVC's Training and Technical Assistance Center offers a 2-day training that provides tools for program managers who plan and implement evaluations. For more information, see www.ovcttac.gov/views/TrainingMaterials/dspProgramEvaluation.cfm. The Bureau of Justice Assistance (BJA) Center for Program Evaluation and Performance Measurement is a user-friendly online tool designed to help state and local practitioners establish performance measurements and conduct evaluations. For more information, see www.bja.gov/evaluation/index.html.

Research Pillar 3: Evidence-Based Practices

First seen in medical and health care settings, evidence-based practices (EBP) are widely considered the integration of the best research evidence with clinical expertise and patient values[7] (or, in victim services, with victim, survivor, and client values). This practical methodology is enthusiastically promoted and adopted by professionals in many fields, including social services, education, and the criminal justice system. For example, the Community Preventive Services Task Force, appointed by the Director of the Centers for Disease Control and Prevention, provides evidence-based recommendations on public safety and community health topics, including effective school-based programs to prevent violence.[8]

DOJ's Office of Justice Programs (OJP) directly supports the dissemination of evidence-based practices through its Web site, www.CrimeSolutions.gov, a clearinghouse of promising and effective programs that can be adapted for use by state and local practitioners.[9] It currently rates more than 250 criminal and juvenile justice programs as effective, promising, or showing no effects, according to evidence-based research.

While these initiatives and others on the horizon will contribute to a heightened appreciation for evidence-based practices within the victim services field, we need much more research on the effectiveness of the many practices now in use. For example, empirical researchers have identified many services that are effective in helping children, adolescents, and adults after they are exposed to violence as victims or witnesses. At least three expert panels have reviewed treatment interventions for children according to the quality of the evidence base that supports them. From these reviews, three models emerged: trauma-focused cognitive behavioral therapy, abuse-focused cognitive behavioral therapy, and parent-child interaction therapy. Yet despite the apparent consensus among experts, the field has been slow to adopt these interventions. Other practices have some theoretical basis, are widely accepted and used in the field, and have significant anecdotal support in service delivery settings, but have not been subjected to systematic empirical evaluation.

EBP's basic premise, regardless of the field, is to provide transparency, thus assuring the public that the techniques and procedures will provide the best possible outcomes. Increasingly, consumers and funders expect and demand that a treatment, intervention, or service is known to be effective and based on empirical evidence, not offered simply because a practitioner thinks it will work or it has garnered testimonials. In this deficit-reduction environment, it is even more critical that funding support programs that work.

The victim assistance field must take a careful and systematic approach to institutionalizing research as the foundation for all programs and practices, while taking care not to stifle innovation. There simply is not a comprehensive body of EBPs that

vision 21 BEACON

Trauma-focused cognitive behavioral therapy (TF–CBT) (Cohen, Mannarino & Deblinger, 2006), a treatment for children following exposure to violence, is theoretically, clinically, and empirically supported and has been established as a proven practice. Specifically, multiple empirical studies established that children's trauma-related symptoms decrease following TF–CBT. Known as a promising practice, the Triple P Positive Parenting Program (Prinz, Sanders, Shapiro, Whitaker & Lutzker, 2009) has some preliminary empirical evidence as a multilevel family intervention aimed at preventing severe emotional and behavioral concerns in children at risk for child maltreatment.

[7] Institute of Medicine, *Crossing the Quality Chasm: A New Health System for the 21st Century* (Washington, DC: National Academy Press, 2001: 147), www.iom.edu/Reports/2001/Crossing-the-Quality-Chasm-A-New-Health-System-for-the-21st-Century.aspx (accessed May 11, 2012).

[8] For more information, see www.thecommunityguide.org/violence/index.html.

[9] For more information, see www.crimesolutions.gov/default.aspx.

practitioners can draw from for all services and interventions for all victims. We can't be sure how to treat child victims of online pornography, for example, because we know so little about the impact of this crime on its victims. The combination of research with innovative practice may eventually lead to a tested and proven treatment. Practitioners also should not assume that an EBP will be effective in situations other than those for which it was evaluated. For example, evidence-based mental health interventions rooted in Western culture are not always effective when applied to foreign national human trafficking victims or victims with cognitive disabilities. Also, service providers and crime victims in Indian Country report that traditional cultural healing practices, such as sweat lodges and traditional dancing, can help bring victims to emotional and spiritual recovery more effectively than an EBP tested in non-tribal settings.

Challenges

One of the principal challenges in advancing research to improve crime victim services is the lack of communication and collaboration among researchers and practitioners. Practitioners are often unaware of important research studies that could help shape their work. Even when they are aware of research, practitioners may be unable to interpret and apply the findings, which may not be presented in a straightforward, understandable manner. Much of the research published to date lacks a clear explanation of its implications for practice, which further limits the field's ability to translate research into practice.

Given the long-standing and intractable status of this research-to-practice issue, some Vision 21 participants saw the need for a "third party translation center." The center, perhaps composed of professionals who successfully navigate the worlds of research and victim assistance, would work with practitioners to identify strategic, programmatic, and operational issues in practice for researchers to address. It would also work with researchers to translate research findings into pragmatic operational practices. The result would be more focused research that is made more accessible and integrated into field practices, yielding higher-quality services to victims, their families, and their communities.

Improved collaboration and third-party interventions will not lead to advances in the field if basic funding for research is not available. Current victim assistance guidelines governing the use of <u>Victims</u>

Child victims and posttraumatic stress disorder (PTSD). A number of organizations and agencies have issued guidelines for identifying effective practices for treating children and adults who have been exposed to violence. For example, the International Society for Traumatic Stress Studies developed treatment guidelines for PTSD in children (Cohen, Berliner & March, 2000), and the American Academy of Child and Adolescent Psychiatry issues guidelines for assessment and treatment of PTSD (American Academy of Child and Adolescent Psychiatry, 1998).

Several states have developed guidelines for the treatment of child abuse cases. Whereas each set of guidelines varies slightly, treatments typically are considered as either unacceptable or without any support, as a promising practice, or as a well-supported and efficacious treatment.

- ■ *Promising practices* are those that have a sound theoretical basis, have substantial anecdotal literature on their clinical utility, are accepted in clinical practice and appropriate for the treatment of trauma exposure, and have a book or manual that specifies the components of the treatment and how to administer it, but that do not have clinical or empirical evidence indicating substantial risk of harm compared to benefit.

- ■ *Well-supported, efficacious treatments* have the same criteria as promising practices, as well as at least two randomized-controlled treatment outcome studies documenting the treatment to be superior to a comparison treatment, and multiple treatment outcome studies showing that the overall weight of evidence supports the efficacy of the treatment.

of Crime Act (VOCA) of 1984 funding have been interpreted as prohibiting VOCA state administering agencies and their sub-grantees from using VOCA funds for program evaluation. We expect to address the use of VOCA formula funding for program evaluation in an upcoming notice of proposed rulemaking. Using funding for evaluation often requires a tradeoff with funding for basic services. Further, the state agencies that administer VOCA formula funding are limited to using a maximum of 5 percent of their annual grant to cover administrative costs, training, and technical assistance—an amount that can be challenging to cover those activities, let alone allow for systematic, comprehensive evaluation of VOCA-funded programs.

Nevertheless, Vision 21 stakeholders view research as indispensable to the future of the victim services field and to the continued capacity of providers to help crime victims rebuild their lives. They anticipate that using scientifically sound, evidence-based programs and services will become the norm for the 21st century victim service provider, who will play a pivotal role in data collection and program evaluation to bring about the meaningful, lasting transformation of the victim services field. Our field needs policy flexibility and sufficient funding to transform into one that is focused on advocacy and founded on science.

CHAPTER 2
Meeting the Holistic Legal Needs of Crime Victims

Vision 21 Statement

Every state will establish wraparound legal networks that will help ensure that crime victims' rights are enforced and that victims of crime receive the broad range of legal services needed to help rebuild their lives in the aftermath of crime.

Crime Victims' Rights: Promise or Reality?

The vision that launched the victims' rights movement more than 30 years ago arose from a growing awareness and concern that the U.S. criminal justice system neglected or excluded the interests of victims of crime. Attorneys, advocates, criminal justice professionals, and victims themselves began to speak out about the great disparity between the treatment of offenders, who were guaranteed certain rights under the law, and their victims, who were guaranteed few or no rights at all. Sadly, crime victims seeking emotional, physical, or financial support in the wake of victimization quickly found they were on their own.

This harsh reality began to change in the early 1980s. The President's Task Force on Victims of Crime, established by President Ronald W. Reagan in 1982, conducted a nationwide study to assess the treatment of crime victims in the criminal justice system. In its final report, the task force described a "hellish" justice system, focused on offenders

and indifferent to victims' needs.[10] Crime victims endured physical and emotional wounds, costly financial burdens, and an often hostile criminal justice system. Not only did victims face an alarming public tendency to blame them for the crimes, they were often excluded from courtrooms, disrespected by officials, and afforded few rights.[11]

Lois Haight Herrington, who chaired the task force, described the treatment of crime victims in America as "a national disgrace." Victims had been "ignored, mistreated, or blamed" and "handled like photographs or fingerprints—mere evidence to be manipulated at the criminal justice system's convenience." Such insensitivity toward victims, she said, was "not only unjust but unwise" because "without their help, the system cannot hold offenders accountable and stem the tide of future crime."[12]

This landmark report ushered in a new era of hope and promise for crime victims, issuing 68 recommendations to improve the treatment of victims by law enforcement officers and prosecutors, judges and parole boards, lawmakers, and other officials.[13] Within 4 years, 75 percent of the recommendations were adopted.[14] Nationwide, victims gained the rights to receive financial compensation and restitution, be present in court, be heard at sentencing and parole hearings, and receive information about their rights, criminal proceedings, the release or escape of offenders, and available support services. States also began to amend their constitutions to incorporate victims' rights.

---

[10] *President's Task Force on Victims of Crime Final Report*, December 1982, www.ojp.usdoj.gov/ovc/publications/presdntstskforcrprt/welcome.html (accessed April 30, 2012).

[11] National Victims' Constitutional Amendment Network, Victims' Rights Education Project Talking Points Kit, 30, www.nvcap.org/vrep/NVCANVREPTalkingPoints.pdf (accessed November 19, 2012).

[12] Office of Justice Programs, U.S. Department of Justice, *Four Years Later: A Report on the President's Task Force on Victims of Crime* (Washington, DC: GPO, 1986).

[13] *President's Task Force on Victims of Crime Final Report*, December 1982, www.ojp.usdoj.gov/ovc/publications/presdntstskforcrprt/welcome.html (accessed April 30, 2012).

[14] Office of Justice Programs, U.S. Department of Justice, *Four Years Later: A Report on the President's Task Force on Victims of Crime,* (Washington, DC: GPO, 1986).

Since those early days, the Nation has witnessed dramatic progress in the expansion of crime victims' rights, protections, and services—empowering victims to participate in the criminal, civil, and juvenile justice systems, and to be heard at last. At the federal level, the historic passage of VOCA established the Crime Victims Fund (the Fund) to support state victim compensation and local assistance programs. Victims' rights and services were increasingly accepted as an essential component of justice. As the 20th century came to a close, momentum grew to adopt—albeit unsuccessfully—a federal constitutional amendment that would secure victims' rights throughout the United States.

This chapter summarizes the efforts made in the past decade to secure crime victims' rights through federal legislation; the persistence of underreported crime and its impact on victims' rights and services; the difficulties victims still face in navigating the justice system; and ways innovative legal networks can help ensure that victims have a full complement of legal services widely available to address their array of legal needs, whether criminal, civil, or administrative, in the wake of their victimization.

Efforts To Strengthen Enforcement of Victims' Rights

Even though earlier efforts to pass a victims' rights amendment to the Constitution were not successful, the crime victims' rights community advocated successfully for the Crime Victims' Rights Act of 2004 (CVRA). The new law sought to enumerate victims' rights at the federal level, provide mechanisms to seek enforcement of crime victims' rights, and give victims and prosecutors legal standing to assert victims' rights, among other provisions.[15]

Recognizing that enforcement of crime victims' rights was inconsistent, CVRA's bipartisan sponsors understood that rights enforcement would require access to legal services and professional legal representation at tribal, state, and federal levels. CVRA authorized funding for the "support of organizations that provide legal counsel and support services for victims in criminal cases for the enforcement of crime victims' rights."[16] The 2004 legislation built on a demonstration project launched in 2002 by OVC, which developed and evaluated a network of legal clinics that might serve as models for the provision of pro bono legal representation of victims in criminal court.

Funding for the OVC demonstration project ended in 2009. Most of the 12 legal clinics that were established in a handful of states under CVRA and the OVC demonstration project have since significantly decreased operations or closed. The full promise of CVRA was not realized, although the many legal issues facing crime victims remain. Moreover, a system of effective legal services that meets the needs of all crime victims must acknowledge and contend with a sobering reality: the majority of crime victims in the United States never contact law enforcement or step across the threshold of a courtroom.

vision◉BEACON ··

Crime Victims' Legal Assistance Project, a collaboration of Arizona Voice for Crime Victims and the Arizona State University College of Law, represents crime victims pro bono during all criminal proceedings. Law students and volunteer attorneys provide free legal representation, including filing motions, arranging meetings with prosecutors regarding charging decisions, presenting evidence at release hearings, providing legal assistance regarding appropriate plea bargaining, and assisting in presenting evidence at sentencing and victim impact statements, restitution claims, and victim compensation claims.

---

[15] 18 U.S.C. § 3771.

[16] 42 U.S.C. § 10603(d)(4).

The Persistent Dilemma of Underreported Crime

The federal and state frameworks of victims' rights laws are critically important to the crime victims who participate in the criminal justice system. Unfortunately, when only 42 percent of serious violent crimes and 40 percent of property crimes are reported to law enforcement,[17] and only 9 percent of violent crime victims receive direct assistance from a victim services agency,[18] it is clear that millions of crime victims in the United States never experience any form of justice, nor do they benefit from support services that could help them regain a sense of normalcy in their lives.

Numerous emotional barriers appear to play a part in low crime victim reporting rates. Shame, embarrassment, and fear are paramount. Many victims fear retaliation from their perpetrators, disbelief from law enforcement, that their victimization will become public, and the stigma that often accompanies victimization.[19]

Victims often cite lack of trust and confidence in the criminal justice system as a barrier to reporting to law enforcement.[20] Some victims believe that law enforcement will not or cannot do anything on their behalf.[21] Additionally, crime victims who are undocumented immigrants often avoid contact with the criminal justice system for fear of deportation, making them attractive targets for predatory criminals, especially those involved in human trafficking, sexual exploitation, and domestic violence.[22] Others do not report a crime because the perpetrator is also their caretaker—as in cases involving child abuse, elder abuse, or victims with disabilities. Finally, some victims do not understand that the violence perpetrated against them is indeed a crime.[23]

Why are crime victim reporting rates important to a discussion about victims' rights and legal services? Not reporting the crime places severe constraints on the number and type of services a crime victim may access, and may foreclose some options altogether.

vision BEACON

Coalition to Abolish Slavery and Trafficking (CAST) provides linguistically appropriate, culturally sensitive, victim-centered legal services. These services include securing release from detention, preparing for criminal trials, representing clients in removal proceedings, advocating to protect the rights of victim witnesses and to obtain "Continued Presence and Certification," obtaining child custody and restraining orders against traffickers, establishing eligibility for refugee benefits, and filing for T visas for trafficking victims. To date, CAST has a 100 percent track record in successfully obtaining visas on behalf of its clients.

---

[17] Jennifer L. Truman, Criminal Victimization, 2010 (Washington, DC: Bureau of Justice Statistics, 2011: 1), www.bjs.gov/content/pub/pdf/cv10.pdf (accessed December 5, 2011).

[18] Lynn Langton, Use of Victim Service Agencies by Victims of Serious Violent Crime, 1993–2009 (Washington, DC: Bureau of Justice Statistics, 2011:1–15).

[19] Michael R. McCart, Daniel W. Smith, and Genelle K. Sawyer, "Help Seeking Among Victims of Crime: A Review of the Empirical Literature," Journal of Traumatic Stress 23(2) (April 2010): 198–206.

[20] Lawrence W. Sherman, "Trust and Confidence in Criminal Justice," NIJ Journal 248 (2002): 23–31

[21] Patricia Tjaden and Nancy Thoennes, Extent, Nature, and Consequences of Intimate Partner Violence: Findings From the National Violence Against Women Survey (Washington, DC: National Institute of Justice, July 2000), www.ncjrs.gov/pdffiles1/nij/181867.pdf (accessed May 15, 2012).

[22] Jacob Bucher, Michelle Manasse, and Beth Tarasawa, "Undocumented Victims: An Examination of Crimes Against Undocumented Male Migrant Workers," Southwest Journal of Criminal Justice 7(2): 159–179, 2010, http://swacj.org/swjcj/archives/7.2/Bucher%20Article%20(3).pdf (accessed October 23, 2012).

[23] Anita Raj and Jay Silverman, "Violence Against Immigrant Women: The Roles of Culture, Context, and Legal Immigrant Status on Intimate Partner Violence," Violence Against Women, 2002, http://vaw.sagepub.com/content/8/3/367 (accessed October 23, 2012).

For example, crime victims who do not report to and cooperate with law enforcement are not eligible to receive compensation. Ensuring the provision of comprehensive legal services—including the enforcement of victims' rights—requires consideration of the full impact of victim reporting rates and ways to address this problem.

Any serious consideration of crime reporting rates also must acknowledge that—for many crime victims—justice does not always mean having their day in court. This reality is particularly evident when the perpetrator is a family member. Alternatives to incarceration and the traditional criminal justice system, such as restorative justice programs, and peacemaking strategies practiced in many tribal communities, may offer some crime victims a viable path toward personal healing while ensuring that offenders are still held accountable for their crimes.

The victim services community needs a greater understanding of the potential effectiveness of such alternatives while remaining mindful of the potential ongoing concerns for victim safety. OVC is funding a project that will identify, examine, and document effective restorative justice practices, with an emphasis on practices implemented in tribal communities, urban inner-city areas, and those involving youth.[24] OVC anticipates that this assessment will be a first step to addressing the question of whether or not some crime victims, their families, and communities experience greater satisfaction with the achievement of justice through the use of culturally responsive, victim-centered, restorative justice practices.

Encountering the Labyrinth: Victims in the Legal System

Victims of crime all too often face a perplexing maze of coexisting, overlapping, and complex legal issues after their victimization. They must navigate multiple systems (i.e., the criminal, civil, and administrative justice systems), each with its own requirements and processes. One case of victimization may produce myriad legal issues for the victim, including orders of protection, victims' rights enforcement, compensation, employment, housing, home foreclosure, spousal support, and child custody, visitation, and dependency.

Victims of certain types of crime, such as identity theft and other forms of financial fraud, and human trafficking and domestic violence involving undocumented immigrants, may face seemingly insurmountable hurdles. Maneuvering through a virtual labyrinth of systems to address current circumstances and protect against the risk of future victimization is confusing at best, and overwhelming—even traumatizing—at worst.

Serving crime victims in indigenous communities presents a special challenge to all members of the victim service community, particularly providers of legal services. American Indian and Alaska Native populations suffer significantly higher crime rates than the rest of the Nation[25]—a fact that underscores the urgency of finding ways to deliver services more successfully or, in the case of legal assistance, to deliver services at all. Complex jurisdictional issues, along with the cultural diversity of tribes and the basic reality of geography, pose a

vision 21 BEACON ....

Matrimonial and Family Law Unit of the New York Legal Assistance Group provides no-cost legal assistance to low-income battered women. Pro bono attorneys have successfully worked at the city and state levels for legislative and policy changes—including appellate representation—that benefit all domestic violence victims. In one case involving a battered woman who lost custody of her child due to legal procedural mistakes she made, a pro bono attorney helped the victim win a rare reversal in appellate court, thus sending her custody case back for a trial.

---

[24] For more information, see www.ojp.usdoj.gov/ovc/grants/pdftxt/FY2012_Identifying_Culturally_Responsive_Victim.pdf.

[25] *Criminal Victimization, 2010*, National Crime Victimization Survey, Bulletin, September 2011, NCJ 235508 http://bjs.ojp.usdoj.gov/content/pub/pdf/cv10.pdf (accessed August 24, 2012).

significant challenge. Rural Indian reservations may cover vast areas, and the villages of many Alaska Natives may be remote, even inaccessible, in winter. Although sometimes scarce, basic victim assistance and law enforcement are generally more available than legal assistance.

Many crime victims who have a negative experience with the criminal justice system are at greater risk of developing PTSD; physical, mental, and sexual distress; and reduced trust in the justice system.[26] Victims who are promised participatory rights, for example, only to be denied these rights, are generally in an even worse position than if they had not been given the rights at all.[27] Further, victims who are required to undergo demeaning procedures or experience undue delays in legal processes may perceive the criminal justice system as unfair.[28]

It need not be this way. Vision 21 builds on the dream of the field's early pioneers: extending to all crime victims the choice to participate in the criminal justice process, providing each victim with understandable and accurate information about what to expect, and treating each victim with compassion and respect. Under such a system, victims of crime would make fully informed decisions about their post-victimization role and could be more likely to participate willingly in the criminal justice system. For many victims, participation promotes healing, opens access to financial compensation and the potential of restitution, provides them with greater safety and protection, and validates the harm done to them by the offender.[29] If victims feel empowered by their participation in the justice system, they may even experience greater improvement in physical and mental health and quality of life.[30, 31]

Legal Services Networks: An Innovation for the 21st Century

As noted earlier, the enforcement of most crime victims' rights is less relevant to the majority of victims who have little or no involvement with the criminal justice system. For some crime victims, other legal issues may be more pressing. For example, a woman who has been repeatedly battered by her live-in boyfriend and is now facing deportation, eviction from her apartment, separation from her children, or termination from her job will care far more about obtaining legal assistance with these issues than about the violation of her right to be notified about an upcoming court hearing on her criminal case. Eventually, some or all of those needs may be met through a disparate patchwork of resources in the victim assistance community—or there may be no services available at all.

Under the current fragmented system, community-based organizations and system-based agencies typically provide assistance within specifically predefined parameters. System-based services such as those provided through district attorneys' offices or law enforcement departments focus primarily on preparing victims to assist in the investigation and prosecution of their criminal cases. Legal clinics located in a very limited number of jurisdictions represent victims primarily in the enforcement of their legal rights during criminal proceedings.

Some assistance to help victims deal with civil legal issues is available through law school legal clinics, legal services or legal aid offices, and other nonprofit organizations with a focused mission. The Office on Violence Against Women (OVW), U.S. Department of Justice, supports the "Legal

---

[26] Rebecca Campbell and Sheela Raja, 2005, "The Sexual Assault and Secondary Victimization of Female Veterans: Help-Seeking Experiences with Military and Civilian Social Systems." *Psychology of Women Quarterly* 29: 97–106.

[27] Judith Lewis Herman, 2003, "The Mental Health of Crime Victims: Impact of Legal Intervention," *Journal of Traumatic Stress* 16(2): 159–166.

[28] Margret E. Bell et al., 2011, "Battered Women's Perception of Civil and Criminal Court Helpfulness: The Role of Court Outcomes and Processes," *Violence Against Women* 17: 72.

[29] L.B. Cattaneo and L.A. Goodman, 2010, "Through the Lens of Therapeutic Jurisprudence: The Relationship Between Empowerment in the Court System and Well-Being for Intimate Partner Violence Victims," *Journal of Interpersonal Violence* 25(3): 481–502.

[30] Ibid.

[31] National Crime Victim Law Institute. 2010a. "Fundamentals of Victims' Rights: A Brief History of Crime Victims' Rights." NCVLI Working Paper. Portland, OR.

Assistance for Victims (LAV) Program," which provides criminal and civil legal services for victims of domestic violence, sexual assault, dating violence, and stalking throughout the Nation. Community-based victim service agencies also help educate victims about the criminal justice system, but these agencies often focus on specific crimes, such as domestic violence or sexual assault, to the exclusion of the full range of crimes that afflict victims. Often, this support does not involve professional legal representation.

A recent landmark study of California victim/witness assistance centers that serve female victims of domestic violence, sexual assault, and stalking underscored the service gaps in helping victims with legal issues, particularly with access to free legal representation.[32] Conducted by the California Crime Victims Assistance Association, in collaboration with the California District Attorneys Association and the Chief Justice Earl Warren Institute on Law and Social Policy, this statewide research project reported that many violence against women (VAW) programs cited the provision of civil legal assistance—including legal aid referrals and general support for non-criminal protective orders, divorce, and child custody issues—as their greatest service gap.[33] Furthermore, surveyed advocates noted a common disparity in the legal voice that VAW victims have compared to what the primary aggressors/partners may have in civil legal matters, described as the "upper hand" in court.[34]

Compounding the lack of legal representation for crime victims is the absence of a single point of entry through which victims of all types of crime may access services to address the wide range of legal needs they may have as the result of their victimization. Further, the scope and quality of assistance available to any individual victim varies widely from community to community, and finding just the right kind of assistance needed at a particular moment can be difficult, if not impossible, for many victims of crime.

Vision 21 explored the value of addressing victims' multiple issues through a broad and coordinated community network of "wraparound" pro bono legal services that would help victims assert their legal rights and obtain the specialized legal assistance they need. A coordinated, collaborative, and holistic legal response has the potential to serve victims far better through an inherent capacity to provide the type of legal assistance needed at any given time. A network approach would also ensure that victims are connected to community legal resources that can help them address their administrative, civil, and other legal issues. This approach would build on existing federal and state funding streams for different types of legal assistance, leveraging but not duplicating what already exists within a community.

No effort of national scope has been undertaken to support the holistic delivery of comprehensive legal services for victims of crime. Recognizing the need, in 2012, OVC released a competitive grant solicitation to support the development of collaborative networks to support holistic, pro bono legal services to address the full spectrum of legal issues crime victims face.[35] Due to limited discretionary funding, OVC is supporting six demonstration sites under this solicitation. Nevertheless, the projects funded under this initiative will be evaluated fully and have the potential to serve as model programs in the future.

Lack of Research Is an Issue

One of the most enduring challenges in ensuring that victims' rights are enforced is simply how little we know about the true impact of crime victims' rights and the extent to which victims' rights are enforced. Many anecdotal reports about victims' rights not being honored, or victims not receiving the services to which they are entitled, are shared by victim service providers and crime victims alike. There is, however, surprisingly little research examining how victims' rights provisions are implemented, whether victims actually receive the rights and

[32] Heather Wamken, "Violence Against Women Needs Assessment Program," (San Diego, CA: California Crime Victims Assistance Association, February 29, 2012), 17, http://calvictimassistance.com/w4p/wp-content/uploads/2012/03/VAW-study.pdf (accessed June 21, 2012).

[33] Ibid.

[34] Ibid.

[35] Office for Victims of Crime, 2012, "Wraparound Victim Legal Assistance Network Demonstration Project" solicitation, www.ojp.usdoj.gov/ovc/grants/pdftxt/FY2012_WraparoundVictimLegalAssistance.pdf (accessed August 8, 2012).

services to which they are entitled under law, and whether being provided with these rights and services actually increases victims' well-being, cooperation, and satisfaction with the criminal justice system and improves criminal justice system outcomes.

Most of the research on this topic is dated[36] and appears to have been generated by the debate over whether statutes alone were sufficient to protect victims' rights and ensure victims' services. No systematic research was conducted to address the impact of CVRA on victims' rights provided under law, the enforcement of victims' rights, or victims' satisfaction with their treatment by the criminal justice system. There has been some legal analysis of selected cases that suggests the problems identified with statutory approaches to protecting victims' rights still exist, and a Government Accountability Office report documented the existence of continuing problems with CVRA implementation.[37, 38] Sound research needs to provide the foundation for future action to ensure crime victims' rights and provide comprehensive legal services for victims of crime.

Challenges

Despite the accomplishments of the past 30 years in securing victims' rights and addressing their legal needs, challenges remain that prevent victims of crime from fully accessing their legal rights and receiving comprehensive legal services. Wraparound legal services may well be the next wave in the victims' movement, an innovation that would allow victims to emerge from victimization with their dignity intact and a sense of fairness and justice. Although every person encounters the justice system differently, the way victims are treated by justice system practitioners and the degree of control and ownership they can exercise significantly influence their experience. Wraparound legal services offer great potential for addressing the legal needs of crime victims while ensuring that they have a voice in matters of vital interest to them. There are two primary challenges to the expansion of wraparound legal assistance: resource constraints and collaboration.

These efforts inevitably would be resource-intensive, but the advantage of the wraparound model is the recognition that funding and resources exist but have not been linked or coordinated to create a network or continuum of legal services for crime victims. Additional funding, as proposed in the President's 2014 Budget, is needed to establish those linkages in jurisdictions across the country. State VOCA administrators recognize the tremendous potential of comprehensive, wraparound legal assistance and have voiced support for the concept, but do not have resources to support these services.

Additionally, these efforts involve substantial, sustained collaboration across a wide array of agencies, organizations, and jurisdictions to ensure a full complement of legal assistance for victims. As noted elsewhere in this report, the field still struggles with the challenge of collaboration—a challenge made more complex by the increasing demand to move beyond informal partnerships, coalitions, teams, or task forces to the creation and institutionalization of broad, formal, often multijurisdictional, system linkages.

vision**BEACON** ··

VictimLaw is a comprehensive, user-friendly, online database of more than 16,000 victims' rights statutes, tribal laws, constitutional amendments, court rules, administrative code provisions, and case summaries of related court decisions designed for users with different levels of substantive and technological expertise. Developed by NCVC and maintained by OVC's Training and Technical Assistance Center (OVC TTAC), *VictimLaw* helps victim advocates, prosecutors, crime victims, college professors, and others research the ever-growing body of crime victims' rights statutes.

[36] Office for Victims of Crime, *New Directions from the Field: Victims' Rights and Services in the 21st Century*, NCJ 170600 (Washington, DC: U.S. Department of Justice, Office of Justice Programs, 1998), https://www.ncjrs.gov/ovc_archives/directions/pdftxt/direct.pdf

[37] U.S. Government Accountability Office, *Crime Victims' Rights Act: Increasing Awareness, Modifying the Complaint Process, and Enhancing Compliance Monitoring Will Improve Implementation of the Act*, December 2008 (GAO–09–54).

[38] Some members of the victim services field believe that CVRA has not lived up to its potential to date, while others respond that a major contributing issue is that states are not adopting strong rights laws. Thus, disparate justice continues to exist. In fact, a Joint House Resolution proposing a victims' rights amendment to the Constitution of the United States was introduced recently. See H.J.Res.40.IH, 113th Congress, 1st Session.

CHAPTER 3
Extending the Vision: Reaching All Victims of Crime

Vision 21 Statement

All crime victims in the 21st century can readily access a seamless continuum of evidence-based services and support that will allow them to begin physical, emotional, and financial recovery.

Meeting the Needs of All Victims

Multiple, complex challenges prevent the victim assistance field from realizing the common goal of reaching each victim in need of hope and help. New types of crime have emerged and proliferated as a result of changes brought about by technology, globalization, and evolving demographics in our society. Meanwhile, long-standing types of victimization endure, demanding a renewed commitment to action.

Regardless of the enduring or evolving nature of crime, expanding the reach of victim assistance starts with recognizing the pervasiveness of domestic violence, sexual assault, and child maltreatment in this country, and their connection with other types of victimization. VOCA made funding for programs that serve victims of these crimes a priority.[39] It also set as a priority funding for a broad category of underserved victims.[40] Despite the tremendous progress propelled by VOCA, the Violence Against Women Act, and other federal and state legislation, family and sexual violence remain challenges for our society.

Moreover, these victims' needs are not fully met by service providers. During a 24-hour period in September 2011, the annual National Census of

Domestic Violence Services documented 10,581 unmet requests for services, including emergency shelter, housing, transportation, child care, and legal representation. A 2012 national survey by the National Alliance to End Sexual Violence revealed that 50 percent of rape crisis centers have reduced staff in the past year and 65 percent have a waiting list for counseling services.

Numerous studies have documented strong links between child abuse, trauma, and neglect, and a child's mental and physical health. A recent study of children living in a violent, low-income neighborhood who were constantly exposed to violent events such as shootings showed they were 30 times more likely to have learning and behavior problems than children who were not exposed to traumatic events.[41] Society is only beginning to realize the impact of everyday trauma in children's lives and the subsequent need to ensure that all child victims receive trauma-informed care.

The field also struggles to systematically assess and address the historical, institutional, geographic, cultural, and other barriers that prevent many underserved victims from receiving services and support. Stakeholders noted that among those most in need of support are American Indians and Alaska Natives, who experience higher crime rates than any other population in the United States.[42] Resources have been limited on tribal lands, but a renewed focus on public safety and victimization gives hope for improvement. U.S. Attorney General Eric H. Holder, Jr., has declared that DOJ has both "a legal duty and a moral obligation to address violent crime in

---

[39] 42 U.S.C. §10603(a)(2)(A).

[40] 42 U.S.C. §10603(a)(2)(B).

[41] Nadine J. Burke et al., June 2011, "The Impact of Adverse Childhood Experiences on an Urban Pediatric Population," *Child Abuse and Neglect: The International Journal*, 35(6): 408–413.

[42] Office for Victims of Crime, *Using Federal Law To Prosecute Domestic Violence Crimes in Indian Country*, Facilitator's Guide, (Washington, DC, 2012) 9.

Indian Country and to assist tribes in their efforts to provide for safe tribal communities."[43]

Services for some crime victims may be unavailable, inadequate, or difficult to access. Stakeholders identified this as a particular issue with groups such as victims with disabilities, older victims, victims in detention settings, boys and young men of color, runaway and homeless youth, homeless adults, victims in congregate housing such as nursing homes and mental health facilities, and LGBTQ victims. Some of these populations experience higher crime rates than the overall U.S. population, making their need for assistance all the more critical.

Complicating the field's mission is the rise of new victimization issues over the past two decades amid—and sometimes driven by—seismic shifts in demographics, major advances in technology, dynamic socioeconomic trends, and rapid globalization. A brief examination of some of the ensuing challenges follows.

Demographic Shifts

Due to language barriers and cultural norms and expectations, changes in U.S. demographics make it increasingly challenging to deliver services to victims who are immigrants or who have limited English proficiency. Additionally, undocumented immigrant victims who fear deportation or law enforcement may simply not ask for help. Laws in some states that restrict rights and services for undocumented immigrants, even if they are criminally victimized, further complicate the challenges in serving these victims.

In the past decade, Latino and Asian Pacific Islander populations each grew by more than 40 percent; the American Indian and Alaska Native population increased by 39 percent; and Americans 65 years of age and older increased by 15.1 percent—about two-thirds faster than the overall U.S. population (9.7 percent).[44] Over the next 40 years, the U.S. population is likely to grow by a third, including more adults over the age of 65, young and working people, Latino and Asian populations, and people who self-identify as "mixed ethnicity."[45, 46]

Hate Crimes

Hatred born of prejudice and bias almost certainly has motivated criminal acts throughout human history (Gould, 1981). The primary source of data on hate crime is the UCR, which defines a hate crime as "a criminal offense committed against a person, property, or society that is motivated, in whole or in part, by the offender's bias against a race, religion, disability, sexual orientation, or ethnicity/national origin."[47] Individual states vary with regard

vision BEACON

The Florida Coalition Against Domestic Violence developed and distributed FotoNovelas in 20 Florida counties with a heavy concentration of Spanish-speaking migrant communities that have a historical lack of trust in law enforcement, a fear of deportation, and a lack of awareness about domestic violence laws and protections in the United States. These comic book-style publications depict domestic violence using understandable stories and inform victims of available toll free crisis and legal hotline services, shelters, victim advocacy, and legal assistance. Calls for assistance increased more than 200-fold as a result of this outreach.

[43] Attorney General Eric H. Holder, Jr., "Oversight of the Department of Justice" Congressional Testimony, November 18, 2009, www.mainjustice.com/files/2009/11/AG-Holder-Written-Testimony-SJC-111809-DOJ-Oversight-Hearing-FINAL1.pdf (accessed May 31, 2012).

[44] U.S. Census 2010, www.census.gov/2010census/index.php (accessed June 1, 2012).

[45] Joel Kotkin, "What American Demographics Will Look Like in 2050," March 15, 2010, www.joelkotkin.com/content/00188-what-american-demographics-will-look-2050 (accessed May 31, 2012).

[46] Joel Kotkin, "America in 2050—Strength in Diversity," March 19, 2010, www.joelkotkin.com/content/00190-america-2050-strength-diversity (accessed May 31, 2012).

[47] Federal Bureau of Investigation. Hate Crime Statistics, 2009. Washington, DC: U.S. Department of Justice, Federal Bureau of Investigation, November 2010.

to the groups protected under hate crime laws (e.g., gender, gender identity, perceived characteristics, age, association).

Crimes of hate in America are not a vestige of our distant past. Between January 1995 and September 1998, arsonists destroyed more than 200 black churches.[48] In 1998, Americans were horrified by the brutal murder of Matthew Shepard because he was gay and of James Byrd, Jr., because he was African American. These murders highlight the true effects of violent hate crime; they are not directed only at the individual, but are intended to break the spirit of a community—to inflict harm and instill fear.[49] These brutal murders led to the passage of the Matthew Shepard and James Byrd, Jr., Hate Crimes Prevention Act of October 2009.

On August 5, 2012, a lone gunman and self-described white supremacist shot six people and wounded four others at a Sikh temple in Oak Creek, Wisconsin, before fatally shooting himself. U.S. Attorney General Eric H. Holder, Jr., speaking at the memorial service in Oak Creek for the victims of this crime, described the incident as "an act of terrorism, an act of hatred, a hate crime." Sikh rights groups have reported a rise in bias attacks since the September 11 terrorist attacks. The Washington-based Sikh Coalition documented more than 300 cases of violence and discrimination against Sikh Americans in the month following the September 11 attacks, which may be tied to the erroneous confusing of Sikhs with Muslims.[50]

Hate crimes continue to challenge the safety and well-being of people in the United States. The crime victim services field is challenged with identifying the needs of hate crime victims and working diligently to help meet those needs and assist in their recovery.

Human Trafficking

Often referred to as modern-day slavery, human trafficking is a highly profitable crime that remains largely invisible to the American public, despite the passage of federal and state anti-human trafficking legislation and enormous media attention. Traffickers often operate undetected and victims are unlikely to come forward for assistance. Human trafficking is sometimes "hidden in plain sight," challenging law enforcement and service providers alike to identify, rescue, and serve the victims of this "new" crime of human slavery. Victims may not understand that their victimization is a crime or that they have rights and are entitled to assistance.[51] Trafficking victims may be men, women, or children; U.S. citizens; legal permanent residents; or foreign nationals who are forced or coerced into activities such as agricultural labor, begging, servile marriage, domestic servitude, restaurant service, pornography, or prostitution. Under federal and some state laws, minors (under age 18) involved in commercial sex acts are deemed victims of human trafficking, regardless of evidence of force or coercion. All human trafficking victims, both foreign

Safe Horizon's Streetwork Project in New York City provides a safe haven for thousands of homeless and street-involved young people—many the victims of sexual abuse, sex trafficking, and child maltreatment—who can get hot meals, warm showers, clean clothing, medical treatment, and victim services in a supportive and nonjudgmental environment. Each year, this program touches the lives of more than 19,000 young people, distributes more than 45,000 meals, and offers a lifeline to thousands of youth who have no other support systems.

---

[48] www.anzasa.arts.usyd.edu.au/a.j.a.s/Articles/2_08/1FINAL%20MINCHIN2.pdf.

[49] www.whitehouse.gov/the-press-office/remarks-president-reception-commemorating-enactment-matthew-shepard-and-james-byrd-

[50] www.sikhcoalition.org/images/documents/fact%20sheet%20on%20hate%20against%20sikhs%20in%20 20america%20post%209-11%201.pdf.

[51] U.S. Department of State, *Trafficking in Persons Report*, (Washington, DC: U.S. Department of State, June 2011) www.state.gov/j/tip/rls/tiprpt/2011/index.htm (accessed November 19, 2012).

and domestic, face formidable barriers in escaping the bonds of trafficking, accessing services, and achieving a sense of normalcy and self-sufficiency in their lives.

Domestic minor victims of sex trafficking have received heightened attention in the past few years. Frequently abused or neglected as younger children, many have become runaway or "throw-away" youth, making them vulnerable to sexual exploitation through street prostitution and online or other escort services. Many of these children are also trapped in the revolving door of child welfare/ foster care systems, juvenile justice systems, and other systems that do not recognize and address their victimization. All too often, they are viewed as juvenile offenders rather than victims in desperate need of safety, support, and trauma-informed care.

Crimes Against Americans Abroad

Greater numbers of Americans are traveling and working abroad, a phenomenon that is expected to increase in this century. An estimated 6.32 million U.S. citizens reside overseas,[52] not including military service members. Stakeholders identified the need to serve Americans who are victimized abroad, but most victim-serving organizations are unable to assist crime victims overseas. Needed crisis assistance is not always available in foreign countries or on cruise ships in international waters. Nor do all state crime victim compensation funds extend eligibility for compensation of crime-related expenses to Americans who are victimized in foreign countries.

VOCA provides OVC only limited authority to support assistance to victims abroad other than victims of terrorism.

Mass Violence and Disasters

Destruction from terrorism and mass violence, such as the mass shootings that recently occurred at a movie theatre in Aurora, Colorado, and a Sikh temple in Oak Creek, Wisconsin, occurs in a life-shattering instant. Other forms of mass criminal victimization, such as large-scale human trafficking or child sexual abuse cases, may unfold over months or years. Natural disasters may diminish public safety and strain law enforcement capabilities, creating a breeding ground for violent crime and financial fraud. Environmental incidents such as the knowing and wanton disposal of toxic or carcinogenic wastes and the subsequent harm to victims may not be discovered and adjudicated as criminal acts until many years afterward.

Cybercrime

Advances in technology and its widespread use provide new opportunities for perpetration of traditional crimes and the emergence of new ones, including online financial fraud, identity theft, cyber-stalking, sexual exploitation, computer hacking, and corporate data breaches.[53] Cybercrime typically crosses jurisdictional boundaries, sometimes even international borders, and presents extreme challenges in investigating and prosecuting these crimes and providing assistance to victims.[54]

Americans Overseas Domestic Violence Crisis Center. In 2010, OVC funded a demonstration project to provide a continuum of services to American families—military and civilian—experiencing domestic violence overseas. The Americans Overseas Domestic Violence Crisis Center provides domestic violence and child abuse advocacy, tools, and resources to help victims navigate complicated jurisdictional, legal, and social landscapes in order to live free of abuse. Tools include an international toll-free crisis line, 866–US–WOMEN, which is accessible from 175 countries. In 2010, the center received 2,289 crisis calls, e-mails, and live chats on behalf of 481 families in 68 countries.

[52] Association of Americans Resident Overseas, "6.32 Million Americans Abroad Map," www.aaro.org/about-aaro/6m-americans-abroad (accessed November 19, 2012).

[53] For more information on cybercrime, visit the National Cyber Security Alliance at www.staysafeonline.org/.

[54] In 2009, OVC partnered with DOJ's Criminal Division and the National Crime Victim Law Institute to seek justice for Americans victimized by a complex Internet fraud conspiracy based in Romania—the first such initiative of its kind. Prosecution of the perpetrators is ongoing within the Romanian justice system.

The online possession and distribution of pornographic child images presents daunting challenges for law enforcement, prosecutors, and victim service providers. Victims may be "violated" in cyberspace thousands of times and in perpetuity. We know very little about the harm that accrues to these victims. Complex and sometimes conflicting federal case law makes it difficult for courts to apply the laws that govern restitution in child pornography possession and distribution cases. This legal complexity, coupled with the research gap regarding the impact of this crime on its victims, means that victims do not always receive adequate orders of restitution. Even if courts do order restitution, victims experience great difficulty in getting payments from multiple defendants in jurisdictions across the country. Furthermore, most state crime victim compensation funds do not have specific policies regarding the eligibility of child victims of pornography to receive reimbursement for victimization-related expenses. OVC informally polled states during 2011 and 2012 and found that most reported having not received claims from victims of child pornography related to the crime of possession and distribution of their images online, even though these victims would be eligible in most states.

These issues illustrate the kinds of challenges that will continue to confront the criminal justice system and the victim assistance field in the 21st century.

The Challenges of Collaboration

The field has long understood that collaboration and community coordinated responses are integral components of assisting crime victims. Stakeholders resoundingly affirmed that collaboration remains a centerpiece of the victim response—and that the field still struggles to implement it effectively. They noted that effective collaboration in the 21st century has moved beyond that of informal partnerships to one of institutionalizing broad system

and increasingly multijurisdictional linkages. The Full Frame Initiative,[55] a nonprofit advocacy organization that is leading a national charge to align policy, community-based practice, and research to break the cycles of poverty, violence, and trauma, compellingly outlined the field's struggle, declaring that "the bubbles and structures of our fields are often a big part of what needs to change. They can damn us to refine, rather than transform existing practice."

The Building Partnerships for the Protection of Persons with Disabilities Initiative (BPI) in Massachusetts exemplifies this new model of formal collaboration. BPI was forged in response to the horrific abuse of two individuals with disabilities that went unaddressed by several agencies that had received reports of the abuse. Massachusetts linked a broad range of state agencies to ensure that future incidents would not go unnoticed. The partnership involves law enforcement, prosecution, human service agencies, adult protective services, self-advocates, victim service agencies, and other state agencies.[56] It has brought about remarkable system change in the protection of individuals with disabilities and demonstrates what can be done when systems join together to address victimization.

NCVC joined its victim advocacy efforts with those of the National Coalition of Anti-Violence Programs—a national victim advocacy organization and a national alliance of organizations advocating for the rights of LGBTQ individuals. The resulting seminal policy report released in 2010, *Why It Matters: Rethinking Victim Assistance for Lesbian, Gay, Bisexual, Transgender and Queer Victims of Hate Violence and Intimate Partner Violence*,[57] provides one of the first major examinations of hate crimes and intimate partner violence against LGBTQ individuals—and the capacity of the victim services field to serve them.

---

[55] For more information about The Full Frame Initiative, go to www.fullframeinitiative.org.

[56] For more information, see www.buildingpartnershipsma.org/index.htm.

[57] *Why It Matters: Rethinking Victim Assistance for Lesbian, Gay, Bisexual, Transgender and Queer Victims of Hate Violence and Intimate Partner Violence*, National Center for Victims of Crime and National Coalition of Anti-Violence Programs (Washington, DC, 2012). (Accessed at www.ncvc.org, August 20, 2012).

Prevention: An Expanded Role for Victim Services?

Vision 21 stakeholders confirmed the value of prevention in creating safe and healthy communities. They believe that crime victims and victim service providers and advocates have much to contribute to prevention policy and programming. But if the victim services field faces tremendous demands to serve crime victims, why contemplate a larger role in prevention? Stakeholders cited the formidable problems confronting the criminal justice system, including escalating budgets, overcrowded jails and prisons, and high offender recidivism rates, coupled with the lifetime financial and emotional costs related to addressing victims' needs as compelling reasons for this expanded role.

Three Levels of Prevention

The practice framework used widely by the public health and health care fields encompasses three levels of practice: (1) primary prevention, which targets the general public with outreach to create awareness aimed at preventing injury or health conditions such as diabetes from occurring in the first place; (2) secondary prevention, which targets individuals at high risk for developing a particular health problem; and (3) tertiary prevention, which targets individuals who have experienced the problem and need assistance in addressing and/or alleviating it to the degree possible.

Victim service providers are involved in post-crime secondary prevention such as interventions designed to lessen or prevent the re-traumatization that sometimes occurs when victims attempt to navigate through a confusing and sometimes insensitive criminal justice system. Tertiary prevention, a mainstay of victim services practice, often takes the form of safety planning—a specific set of actions, strategies, and resources designed to prevent re-victimization and ensure the safety of the person who has already been victimized. However, service providers rarely have the opportunity to participate in activities focused on the general public to prevent victimization from occurring in the first place; primary prevention is not authorized under VOCA.

Mothers Against Drunk Driving (MADD) is an astonishingly successful model of prevention driven by victims.[58] Candice Lightner founded the nonprofit organization in 1980 after her 13-year-old daughter was killed by a drunk driver. MADD's advocacy and prevention campaigns have transformed society's attitudes and the legal landscape for drunk and drugged driving in this country. MADD also provides direct assistance to victims and survivors of victims of drunk and drugged driving crashes. According to the National Highway Traffic Safety Administration, the number of deaths tied to drunk driving has been cut in half since MADD was founded in 1980.[59]

vision 21 BEACON

The International Rescue Committee of Washington State, a 2004 OVC grantee, provides support and services for foreign national victims of sex and labor trafficking. With that funding, the Washington Anti-Trafficking Response Network (WARN) was formed. This collaboration partners with a comprehensive array of service providers as well as local, state, and federal agencies. WARN receives referrals from a host of governmental and nongovernmental agencies such as domestic violence shelters, Volunteer Advocates for Immigrant Justice, Planned Parenthood, U.S. Immigration and Customs Enforcement, and the National Human Trafficking Center. WARN has been successful in assisting human trafficking victims with establishing safe accommodations, obtaining T visas, and achieving self-sufficiency.

---

[58] For more information, see www.madd.org/.

[59] National Highway Traffic Safety Administration FARS data, 2011, www.madd.org/statistics/.

Challenges

Crime victims' access to services is curtailed by a host of complicating factors such as social isolation; fear of stigma; poverty; jurisdictional issues; geography; cultural, language, or communication barriers; immigration status; mistrust of the criminal justice system; fear of retribution; substance abuse; abuse by a family member or caregiver; and homelessness. Some victims still encounter attitudes that regard them as less than deserving victims whose behavior may have contributed to their victimization.

The traditional model of service delivery is increasingly less viable in the 21st century. Victims are still expected to come to a particular location, at a specific time, to meet with a specific service provider. Flexible and innovative service models are emerging but they are not yet standard practice. VOCA limitations, such as the lack of authority to serve some victims at the national and international levels, sometimes hinder innovation.

The field will continue to push for a larger role in primary prevention. Although many in the field would welcome this expanded role, numerous barriers preclude a systematic integration of prevention into the mission of victim service organizations, notably VOCA statutory restrictions, followed by a lack of technical expertise, funding, and staff.

The insufficiency of some resources (e.g., staffing, training and technical assistance, technology) impedes progress. The field needs these resources to drive innovation, increase the efficacy of services, and move from a position of collaborative efforts to one of institutionalized system linkages that provide a seamless, efficient continuum of services for victims. Although we grapple with understanding how many crimes are committed, how many are reported, and how many victims struggle alone to overcome the impact of crime, we do know that victim service providers are working hard to keep their doors open so that victims have somewhere to go for help. The victim assistance field must have an infusion of research and policy changes to drive progress, as well as additional resources as requested in the President's 2014 Budget.

CHAPTER 4
Serving Crime Victims in the Digital Age

Vision 21 Statement

As the 21st century progresses, the victim services field will integrate innovative technologies into its operations, fostering accountability and operational efficiency and ensuring that victims of crime will have streamlined access to services regardless of location, socioeconomic status, and other traditional barriers.

The Impact of the Digital Age

As the 21st century advances, technology continues to transform nearly every aspect of daily life. Americans, along with most of the world, have enthusiastically accepted a host of technological innovations—and eagerly embraced the promise of more—in the name of efficiency and ease. Today's technologies offer new ways to access information, reach out to friends and family, pursue business interests, enjoy entertainment, and engage in social issues, all without leaving home.

These statistics underscore the degree to which Americans rely on communications technologies:

- Eighty-five percent of men and 85 percent of women now use the Internet.[60]

- Eighty-eight percent of Americans have a cell phone, 57 percent have a laptop, 19 percent own an e-book reader, and 19 percent have a tablet computer.[61]

- Nearly half (46 percent) of American adults own Smartphones—more than those who own more basic mobile/cell phones (41 percent).[62]

- By the end of 2012, the number of mobile devices was expected to exceed the number of people on the planet.[63]

The remarkable popularity of online and mobile technology represents an unparalleled opportunity for any industry or profession that cares to harness its power and reach, and victim services is no exception. The victim services field can leverage current technologies to transform itself into a more responsive, efficient, and accessible resource for crime victims throughout the Nation. As countless users of emergency hotlines are already aware, incorporating technology into victim assistance means saving, protecting, and healing human lives.

The need to build an infrastructure that can provide broad access to information and services is being recognized at the highest levels. To increase the Federal Government's capacity to deliver high-quality services to the American people through technology, President Obama recently ordered all government agencies to offer more services through mobile devices within 12 months.[64] This innovative strategy calls for federal agencies "to be ready to deliver and receive digital information and services anytime, anywhere, and on any device."[65]

---

[60] August Tracking Survey" conducted July 16–August 7, 2012, by the Pew Research Center's Internet & American Life Project, www.pewinternet.org/Static-Pages/Trend-Data-(Adults)/Whos-Online.aspx (accessed November 19, 2012).

[61] Pew Research Center's Internet & American Life Project surveys, www.pewinternet.org/Trend-Data-(Adults)/Device-Ownership.aspx (accessed November 19, 2012).

[62] Aaron Smith, "46% of American Adults are Smartphone Owners," (Washington, DC: Pew Research Center's Internet & American Life Project, March 2012).

[63] Cisco, "Cisco Visual Networking Index: Global Mobile Data Traffic Forecast Update, 2011–2016," 3, www.cisco.com/en/US/solutions/collateral/ns341/ns525/ns537/ns705/ns827/white_paper_c11-520862.pdf (accessed November 19, 2012).

[64] Executive Office of the President of the United States, "Digital Government: Building a 21st Century Platform to Better Serve the American People," (Washington, DC: The White House, May 23, 2012). www.whitehouse.gov/sites/default/files/omb/egov/digital-government/digital-government.html (accessed July 5, 2012).

[65] Ibid.

The Power and Potential To Transform Victim Services

Vision 21 participants recommended infusing technology into all aspects of operations and practices, rather than applying it as an adjunct activity to already overburdened programs. Adding one cutting-edge application to a victim service program is a single step in the right direction, but our goal is more ambitious—namely, the transformation of the entire victim services field.

There is a role for technology in virtually every aspect of victim service delivery. In addition to helping the field carry out its primary mission of serving victims, technology can streamline its overall operations. For example, innovative systems can relieve the administrative and reporting burdens associated with multiple funding streams and different standards for accountability. In addition, as many practitioners know, digital communications can broaden access to training and technical assistance, conserving scarce resources while continuing to build professional capacity throughout the field. OVC TTAC has online curricula available through its training center, as well as information about the availability of training on demand and technical assistance.

In this chapter, we discuss some of the opportunities and challenges we face in using current and emerging online technologies to strengthen the field across the entire spectrum of its programs and activities, including direct services, workforce development and training, community outreach and education (including social media), and management and administration.

Online Technologies Serving Victims of Crime

The increased use of online technologies has the potential to greatly expand victim services through personalized and user-friendly applications that facilitate interaction among users and allow for broader and faster information sharing. Social networks, blogs, and RSS feeds deliver regularly updated content directly to online users. Podcasting and video sharing enable victim service providers to continually reach victims with enriched information. Videoconferencing using real-time audio and video technology services, administered through a secure, encrypted connection, can deliver confidential, face-to-face assistance.

Agency Web sites are becoming an increasingly popular tool for disseminating information and services to crime victims. Many agencies have user-friendly sites that help victims access mental health services and other referrals, contact victim support groups, and seek crisis intervention support. Sites can also offer information about specific victimization issues, including victims' rights, safety planning, and navigating the criminal justice process. There are many outstanding Web sites providing much-needed information to victims; however, they are not yet the norm. Further effort is needed to build and refine sites that harness the potential of online technology to serve all crime victims.

Uses in Criminal Justice and Corrections

State and federal corrections institutions use online and automated digital victim notification systems

RAINN's National Sexual Assault Online Hotline, the Nation's first secure Web-based hotline service, provides live and confidential online support to victims around the clock. The anonymous hotline is based on popular instant messaging technology in order to effectively reach young people who are reluctant or unable to pick up the phone or seek services in person. Initial evaluation information from a volunteer survey suggests that the model is viable and effective.

to apprise crime victims and survivors of the status of offenders. A note of caution: refining and improving the use of technology for victim notification systems must take into account issues of victim privacy, security, and safety, in addition to system expediency and efficiency.

In the courtroom, the Denver District Attorney's Office integrates videoconferencing into criminal trials to save money in time and travel expenses for witnesses. Videoconferencing technology allows users to communicate with peers by voice, video, and instant messaging over the Internet. Using this type of online service, often referred to as an "Internet telephone," the office streams expert testimony shown in real time through a monitor into courtrooms.

The Advent and Advantages of Telemedicine in Service Delivery

Telemedicine is the use of telecommunication and information technologies to provide health care from a distance. In a noteworthy example of its successful application, the University of Texas Medical Branch built eight virtual physician studios along with telemedicine stations, enabling health professionals to conduct more than 200 remote medical exams daily.[66] Among those served are inmates of Texas state prisons, who receive quality health care without the security risks and expenses of traveling to a doctor's office. This integration of videoconferencing with electronic medical records, proven disease management protocols, and tele-monitoring has significantly decreased costs while increasing access to care, with improved health outcomes for patients.[67]

This same technology shows great promise for delivering services to hard-to-reach victim populations. Victims in rural areas typically face transportation and other logistical barriers and a lack of qualified service professionals. Multiple jurisdictional

barriers may impede tribal victims' access to quality services. Victims with disabilities often must surmount physical barriers to access care and support. Technology can not only significantly increase access to services for these populations, but the immediacy that online services offer may prompt more victims to take advantage of services.

Technology also offers exciting possibilities for filling critical gaps in victim services. Programs such as Sexual Assault Nurse Examiners (SANEs) or Sexual Assault Forensic Examiners (SAFEs) that provide forensic examinations of sexual assault victims contribute to higher prosecution and conviction rates[68] and yield better outcomes for victims. Too frequently, however, communities do not have access to these specially trained professionals, with rural and tribal populations particularly likely to be shortchanged.

In response to this critical service gap, OVC and the National Institute of Justice (NIJ) are supporting the development of an innovative telemedicine center that will provide less experienced forensic examiners with expert technical guidance when conducting sexual assault forensic examinations. Successfully used for pediatric exams, this project will support and evaluate the impact of this concept for use in adult sexual assault medical-forensic exams at four pilot sites.[69]

Online technologies offer many advantages: many are cost-effective (although upfront costs can be prohibitive for budget-strapped agencies), have built-in features that help maintain confidentiality, and accommodate different lifestyles and technological abilities. They also offer a major advantage in an era of rapidly changing demographics, as online content and interactions may be easily adapted to respond to the race, ethnicity, language, age, and gender of diverse users, helping us address the expanding need for linguistically and culturally appropriate services more efficiently than ever before.

---

[66] Alexander H. Vo, Ph.D., *The Telehealth Promise: Better Health Care and Cost Savings for the 21st Century* (Galveston, Texas, AT&T Center for Telehealth Research and Policy, Electronic Health Network, University of Texas Medical Branch, May 2008), 1, http://telehealth.utmb.edu/presentations/The%20Telehealth%20Promise-Better%20Health%20Care%20and%20Cost%20Savings%20for%20the%2021st%20Century.pdf (accessed July 5, 2012).

[67] Ibid.

[68] Phil Bulman, "Increasing Sexual Assault Prosecution Rates," *NIJ Journal* 264.

[69] Solicitation available at www.ojp.usdoj.gov/ovc/grants/pdftxt/FY2012_SexualAssaultForensicMedical.pdf.

Contributions to Workforce Development and Training

Maintaining a competent victim service workforce in the face of inadequate workforce development and training budgets is profoundly challenging. The nature and capabilities of online technology make it a growing and increasingly accepted way to provide continuing education to victim service providers. OVC, for example, conducts free monthly Web Forums that feature national experts on a broad range of current issues, in addition to the online curricula available through OVC TTAC. The University of Georgia Center for Continuing Education offers an intensive 42-hour, 7-week online victim advocacy certificate program, designed to qualify students to provide assistance to crime victims.

Online training offers many advantages over in-person training, allowing employees and volunteers to learn without leaving the workplace and to repeat difficult parts of a curriculum at their own pace. The elimination of travel time and expenses is also a boon to agencies facing budget restrictions.

Online training can also enhance collaboration by bringing different disciplines together for cross-training. It may be far more convenient and less expensive, for example, for a police detective who works on cold cases to give a presentation and answer questions from victim service providers through a webinar, from the convenience of his own office, than to travel across the country to give the presentation at a conference.

Community Outreach and Education

Victim services organizations and providers understand the importance of ongoing community outreach and education. Local residents need to be aware of the existence of support agencies in their community and the range of services provided, so that they know where to turn in times of need. Effective community outreach and education can also help victims and families efficiently navigate the criminal justice system and reduce the anxiety of participating in that system.

The Denver District Attorney's Office, for example, is developing a self-advocacy tool to help crime victims educate themselves, manage information, and achieve a better understanding of the legal process—sometimes in the midst of their post-victimization trauma. Victims often experience intense emotions and reactions following a crime, and the justice system can be confusing and overwhelming, leading to yet more stress and possible disengagement. The self-advocacy tool could counter these negative reactions with concise, easily accessible information to equip victims with practical knowledge, including descriptions of agency roles and locations; questions to ask prosecutors, victim advocates, and others; and terms commonly used in the judicial system. The tool will be available as an application for use on smartphones, tablet computers, handheld mobile devices, and personal computers.

TF–CBT Web, an online, self-directed multimedia course, trains mental health professionals in *trauma-focused cognitive behavioral therapy*, an evidence-based treatment approach shown to help children, adolescents, and their caretakers overcome trauma-related difficulties. Hosted by the Medical University of South Carolina, this Web-based course has been used by more than 100,000 registered learners, who report significant knowledge gains and increased use of TF–CBT with child victims after taking the online training.

Online Communities Give Victims a Voice

Some Web sites have incorporated victims' voices in order to reach out to crime victims in an effective and nonintrusive manner. The Voices and Faces Project, a nonprofit organization created to share the names, faces, and stories of survivors of sexual violence, operates a popular Web site that allows survivors to read the stories of others who have lived through rape and abuse, and to share their own stories through a digital, confidential online survey. This resource is particularly critical for those who may not have access to such stories in any other way. Creating a virtual online community where victims can testify about their own experiences can provide powerful healing benefits for those who have lived through such violence.[70]

The Limitless Possibilities of Social Media

Social media are opening up enormous opportunities for community outreach and education. We know that 86 percent of white adults, 86 percent of African American adults, and 80 percent of Latino adults use the Internet.[71] Additionally, 64 percent of white adults, 68 percent of African American adults, and 72 percent of Latino adults use social networking sites.[72] The usage rates are even higher for young people ages 12–17, with white youth at 97 percent, African American youth at 95 percent, and Hispanic youth at 88 percent.[73] An estimated 80 percent of all young people regularly use social media sites as an integral part of their lives.[74] This usage data underscores how important it is for the victim services field to fully leverage the powerful influence of social media and social networking sites to reach and support victims of crime.

Not only are social media extremely fast and efficient in disseminating information to large populations, they may serve as the primary means of communicating in the aftermath of major disasters. After the 2011 earthquake in Japan and the devastating tornadoes in the midwestern United States, when all other communication systems broke down, social media became the primary means of communication for getting help to victims and locating missing persons. It is likely that social media will play an even more extensive role in reaching victims or potential victims when quick response is critical before, during, or after natural or man-made disasters and other types of emergencies. Use of social media does not mean the demise of face-to-face victim services and support, of course, but social media communications have the potential to increase demand for invaluable services by raising awareness of their existence.

Management and Administrative Tasks

Technology offers the victim services field a wide range of opportunities to increase its efficiency and accountability. Harnessing technology to develop budgets, maintain administrative records, and track expenditures can help the field serve victims more efficiently and allow for greater cross-statistical analysis.

Program Evaluation and Data Collection

As program evaluation and the development of EBPs become the professional standard for the victim services field, agency managers will increasingly turn to data-collecting technology to help

[70] The Voices and Faces Project: Survivor Stories, www.voicesandfaces.org/survivor.asp (accessed August 21, 2012).

[71] Tracking Survey (August 2012), Pew Research Center's Internet & American Life Project, www.pewinternet.org/Static-Pages/Trend-Data-(Adults)/Whos-Online.aspx (accessed November 19, 2012).

[72] Pew Internet: Social Networking (full detail), www.pewinternet.org/Commentary/2012/March/Pew-Internet-Social-Networking-full-detail.aspx (accessed November 19, 2012).

[73] 2011 Parent-Teen Digital Citizenship Survey, conducted April 19–July 24, 2011, by Pew Research Center's Internet & American Life Project, www.pewinternet.org/Press-Releases/2010/Social-Media-and-Young-Adults.aspx (accessed November 19, 2012).

[74] July 2011 Survey Data. Pew Research Center's Internet & American Life Project, www.pewinternet.org/~/media/Files/Presentations/2012/June/Teens%20Kindness%20Cruelty_NCMEC_WorkingGroup_talk_Lenhart_060512_PDF.pdf (accessed March 7, 2013).

them analyze the measurable impact of victim services. Agencies will be able to electronically generate grant reports for federal, state, and private funders. Greater numbers of victim service agencies will administer and tally the results of online client satisfaction surveys. Technology can also streamline administrative responsibilities, including data collection, which will become routine, automated, and fully integrated into overall operations.

Grant Management

With limited financial resources and administrative staffing support, many in the victim services field find the grant management process to be tedious and burdensome. Technology could transform this present-day reality through the establishment of a uniform electronic system that combines case management tools with functions for preparing grant reports and tracking data. Vision 21 foresees funders and victim service organizations working together to determine consistent terms, measurements, and types of data to be collected that could be used by the entire field and institutionalized through an online system.

Fundraising

More and more nonprofit organizations are turning to the Internet to support their fundraising efforts through Web site donations, e-mail appeals and requests, event registrations, contributions, and other activities. Online giving has grown significantly—with more than 20 percent of adult Internet users saying they have given an online charitable donation—and offers victim services agencies a unique opportunity to increase their revenue streams by building online relationships and expanding their community of donors.[75]

Challenges

Despite impressive pockets of progress in fully integrating technology into the victim services field today, most victim service providers recognize that they lack the ability to fully embrace the unlimited potential that technology offers. Critical factors that must be considered are victims' safety, privacy, and confidentiality, and the evolving nature of technology and subsequent need for new and better tools.

Safety Implications

We must carefully consider the ethical and safety challenges that accompany the use of technology, given the sensitive nature of victim services work and the need for privacy and confidentiality. Online technologies can present serious security issues. A stalking victim whose computer has been hacked may be vulnerable to additional harm from her stalker. An automated digital media system used to notify a victim of a change in an offender's status could fail to reach the victim in time to prevent emotional trauma.

Technology must be used as a tool, not a driver, when interacting with victims. Integrating victims' voices into the conversation about what works and what doesn't is critical for success. The Voices and Faces Project described earlier is effective because,

vision BEACON

Washington State InfoNet, launched by the state's Office of Crime Victims Advocacy and Department of Social and Health Services Children's Administration, is a Web-based data collection system that includes clients served and services provided every day by more than 130 victim service agencies in the state. The system automatically generates more than 30 different types of standard reports, and users also have the ability to request custom reports. Agencies throughout the state have used data from this system for responding to grant solicitations, analyzing staff workloads, conducting client outreach, preparing presentations, and preparing grant reports for both local and private funders.

---

[75] Real Time Charitable Giving—Key Findings, January 12, 2012, Pew Research Center's Internet & American Life Project, www.pewinternet.org/Reports/2012/MobileGiving/Key-Findings.aspx (accessed November 19, 2012).

although online technology is a tool for survivors to share their stories, project administrators have been vigilant in observing privacy protocols and weighing ethical concerns inherent in public story sharing. Ultimately, each new technology-based initiative must be developed with input from privacy experts and the victim population that will be served.

Resource Constraints

Many victim service providers lack the requisite technological expertise, funding, or training on how to maximize technology as a tool for serving victims. Keeping up with current trends and hardware is a challenge for administrators, while upgrading software is expensive in both equipment and staffing. Although they understand the great potential of technology, most organizations are forced to consign technology upgrades to a second or third tier of financial priority. Further, grant funding seldom allows for or provides support for needed technology. Many tribal service providers face additional technological challenges, including inadequate or nonexistent access to the Internet.

The acquisition and maintenance of needed technology systems may also become more resource intensive. For example, the Rape, Abuse & Incest National Network (RAINN), which operates an online hotline through a national network of participating providers, reports that sexual assault victims now spend more time participating in online counseling sessions than they did previously on the organization's long-standing telephone hotline. RAINN officials offer a balanced assessment on using technology to serve victims: although it can be a cost-effective solution to making assistance more accessible, a significant amount of research, technology development, and training is required to provide high-quality care in an online or mobile environment. RAINN recommends that any organi-

zation considering providing victim services online should plan an ongoing assessment of applicable laws, technology solutions, limitations, staffing capacity, and training resources.[76]

Online service providers often find that victims who reach out online have complex issues that require extensive staff expertise and more resources than traditional support services. They may be individuals who would never access telephone or in-person services, so adding an online service capability enables providers to assist some of the most isolated and vulnerable crime victims. Younger victims, in particular, increasingly prefer online services to telephone or face-to-face assistance.[77]

Currently, however, the existing funding restrictions on the mandated uses of VOCA monies set forth decades ago pose a significant challenge to the field's increased use of modern technologies to enhance victim services. For example, states and territories may use no more than 5 percent of their annual VOCA formula grants to administer their compensation and assistance programs and provide technical assistance and training (itself uniquely suited to online delivery systems). As a result, scant funds are available for developing the technological infrastructure and innovation that is desperately needed to advance the provision of services, reach more victims effectively, and reduce the administrative and reporting burdens that are increasingly hampering the field's ability to carry out its mission.

To provide increased access to services to more victims in the 21st century, we must provide the victim services field with the ability to adapt and integrate technology into everyday practice. We must enable victim service providers to become early adopters of technology and give them the capacity to respond to its rapid evolution.

---

[76] Issues to consider in undertaking provision of services online, e-mail from Jennifer Marsh, Rape, Abuse, and Incest National Network (RAINN) Hotline and Affiliate Services Director, July 30, 2012.

[77] Ibid.

CHAPTER 5
Building Capacity To Serve All Victims

Vision 21 Statement

The victim services field will develop and institutionalize capacity to reach and serve all crime victims in need of help and support in the 21st century.

Capacity To Serve Victims in the 21st Century

Vision 21 posed a key question to the field about existing capacity: Is the current network of local, state, tribal, and national organizations, agencies, and institutions sufficient to serve crime victims in the 21st century? For nearly 2 years, OVC worked with crime victims, our project partners, and countless others in the victim assistance and other fields to answer this question. We studied the available research, pondered our role and that of other disciplines, assessed the adequacy of funding, and examined a host of topics, including VOCA and implementing guidelines, diversity in the field, jurisdictional issues, enforcement of victims' rights and access to legal assistance, the use of technology, the availability of training and technology, and the evidence base of our programs and practices. We looked at the victimization that endures in our Nation, including domestic violence, sexual assault,

and child abuse, as well as emerging crimes like human trafficking and financial fraud.

When we finished, we knew the answer to our question: the field lacks the capacity to meet the challenges of the 21st century—not for a lack of will, or passion, or vision—and we must chart a new direction for our future work. We cannot continue to do more of the same and expect that "things will get better" because our cause is just. We described many of the challenges facing the victim assistance field in the past four chapters. This chapter describes what capacity should look like in the 21st century and some of the infrastructure issues that must be overcome.

The Building Blocks of Organizational Capacity

Once again, the lack of research hindered this exploration; stakeholders shared much anecdotal data but scientific, peer-reviewed studies on victim assistance organizational capacity are largely absent. An analysis of capacity should capture baseline data on types and amounts of funding; staff expertise and diversity; salaries and benefits; the use of volunteers; access to state-of-the-art technology, training, and technical assistance; effectiveness

---

vision ⊕ BEACON ....

Coalition to Abolish Slavery & Trafficking (CAST) was established in the wake of the 1995 law enforcement raid of the El Monte sweatshop in Los Angeles, California, where 72 Thai garment workers were enslaved for 8 years. A group of concerned community activists realized something needed to be done to address the re-emergence of slavery. CAST received a small grant from OVC in 1998, the first federal grant to fund services for victims of human trafficking in this country. At that time, CAST lacked the capacity to administer the grant and Little Tokyo Service Center served as its fiscal agent. Today, CAST is an established multiethnic, multilingual organization with an annual budget of $2.4 million that provides intensive case management, comprehensive services, and advocacy for human trafficking survivors. CAST has grown from its grassroots origin to an organization that has been recognized nationally and internationally for its efforts to mobilize communities against human trafficking and provide services and access to justice for its victims.

---

of collaboration and outreach initiatives; and the systematic use of strategic planning, evidence-based practices, and program evaluation. Nor is there much empirical data on the efficacy of collaboration and public outreach efforts at any level of the field. All of these components factor into the capacity to serve crime victims through a cohesive response network throughout the Nation.

To begin to address this research gap, in 2012, OVC provided funding for BJS to begin the development of a statistical system to collect detailed data on services provided to crime victims based on the records of victim assistance organizations and to study the service infrastructure of those organizations. OVC and OVW will work closely with BJS, NCVC, and the RAND Corporation to ensure that data is captured on victims who are served and those who are not, the kinds of services provided and their duration and cost, and the funding sources for various types of services. This statistical system will also capture, for the first time, comprehensive data on the service infrastructure of victim assistance organizations, such as the type of organization; all sources of funding and subsequent reporting requirements; use of standards; access to training and technical assistance; use of technology; number of paid staff and volunteers; salaries, wages, and benefits; and collaboration, public awareness, and outreach efforts.

Strategic planning. Stakeholders identified strategic planning as the cornerstone of organizational capacity. Although it did not address the victim assistance field specifically, research indicates that organizations that tackle high-level questions of mission, vision, and goals have the greatest social impact.[78] Not surprisingly, victim assistance organizations are ill-positioned to define and carry out a strategic plan when they struggle day to day to keep their doors open. Nor have OVC, other federal agencies, state VOCA administering agencies, and national organizations systematically and continuously worked together to drive strategic planning at the national level. The barriers are the same: limited time and funding, lack of consistent

leadership to drive momentum, inadequate staffing to support the process, and a failure of consensus on key goals. The field has paid a price for its less-than-unified strategic efforts. Strategic planning is invaluable to identifying more diversified sources of funding and recruiting a board of directors with the vision and skills to align resources with the mission and goals of the organization. Victim assistance and advocacy groups at the local, state, and national levels should unite their strategic planning efforts to forge a strong and cohesive national network of victim assistance. Many stakeholders suggested continuing Vision 21 as one way to enhance momentum and unify efforts.

Research. There is no successful strategic planning without empirical data. Organizations must understand overall trends in victimization, help-seeking behavior of crime victims, and the efficacy of their programs and practices. Limited research is available on victimization incidence and prevalence rates; victimization reporting on national, state, and community levels; and the help-seeking behavior of many victims, particularly those of emerging types of victimization. Requesting additional funding to respond to the growing and diverse needs of 21st century crime victims, as the President's 2014 Budget does, ultimately must be tied to a willingness to embrace of higher standards of accountability. Adapting EBPs and monitoring, measuring, and evaluating performance must become part of the field's DNA. Managers and staff must acquire the technical expertise to ensure their programs are victim-centered, accountable, and evidence-based.

Stakeholders also lamented the lack of electronic case management systems that could ease the burden of data collection and report generation. State and federal agencies that administer victim assistance funding have a responsibility to provide training, technical assistance, and programmatic incentives to foster these efforts. Stakeholders consistently talked about the need for federal and state agencies to work together to establish standardized benchmarks and subsequent reporting requirements for grant funding recipients.

---

[78] McKinsey & Company, 2001, *Effective Capacity Building in Nonprofit Organizations,* Reston, VA: Venture Philanthropy Partners, www.vppartners.org/sites/default/files/reports/full_rpt.pdf (accessed August 30, 2011).

Human Resource Issues

Human resources—the collective capabilities, experiences, potential, and commitment of an organization's board of directors, management team, staff, and volunteers—are the lifeblood of every organization.

Salaries. In the victim services field, staff pay and benefits are often abysmally low.[79] Stakeholders talked about hiring freezes and staff reductions driven by severe state and local budget cuts. Many programs cannot pay competitive wages or provide good benefits or cost-of-living increases. Deliberate efforts must be made to recognize the professionalism of service providers and ensure that compensation is commensurate with their education, experience, and skill level in order to recruit and retain a diverse and highly competent workforce.

Professional development, support, and training. Professional development and training should be institutionalized, including coaching, mentoring, meaningful performance appraisals, and leadership opportunities. VOCA limitations on the administrative use of formula funding limit the ability of state administering agencies to provide state-of-the-art, readily accessible training and technical assistance for service providers. Victim service providers perform one of society's toughest jobs; too frequently the need for self-care is subsumed in a culture

focused on crisis and day-to-day survival. OVC and other federal agencies must work with states to solve the issue of provider access to training, technical assistance, and professional development and support.

Diversity. Most Vision 21 stakeholders acknowledged that the field still struggles with demographic diversity—minorities, men, and other populations are still not adequately represented in the ranks of the victim assistance field, especially in leadership positions. Cultural competency training, a commitment to antidiscrimination policies, and compliance with the Americans with Disabilities Act, the Civil Rights Act, and other laws that promote equal treatment are foundational steps to progress, but they are not sufficient. The field should study the successes of other fields and disciplines and integrate the goal of greater diversity into strategic planning efforts.

Resources. Resources continue to pose a major challenge to serving more victims. Nonprofit organizations report declining revenue from donors, funders, and endowments.[80] The annual unpredictability of funding challenges programs' ability to plan toward medium and long-term horizons. While acknowledging the difficult fiscal environment, both Congress and the Administration have supported incremental increases in the annual

vision BEACON

The Tennessee Office of Criminal Justice Programs systematically collects and analyzes data through its *S.T.O.P. Violence Against Women Implementation Plan.* It assesses the incidence of domestic violence, sexual assault, stalking, and dating violence in Tennessee[1, 2] and uses population demographics and other data to highlight the areas of greatest need. The state reports that the systematic use of information is helpful in guiding resource allocation and programming decisions. It published the *Managing for Results Guidebook: A Logical Approach for Program Design, Outcome Measurement and Process Evaluation* for S.T.O.P., VOCA, and other victim assistance grantees at the community level. This how-to manual provides victim service agencies with practical guidance on assessing a program's real impact in the community.[3]

[1] Provided under the federal Violence Against Women Act, S.T.O.P. Violence Against Women Act (S.T.O.P. VAWA) Grants improve the criminal justice system's response to violence against women, to securing safety for women, and to holding offenders accountable. S.T.O.P. VAWA grants are provided to law enforcement, prosecution, courts, and victim services programs.

[2] Tennessee Office of Criminal Justice Programs, "S.T.O.P. Violence Against Women Implementation Plan: 2010, 2011, 2012," (Nashville, TN: Department of Finance and Administration, October 2010), www.tn.gov/finance/adm/ocjp/documents/STOPImplementationPlan20102012Final.pdf (accessed May 28, 2012).

[3] For more information, see www.performancevistas.org/TNPerfMeasurementPrimer.pdf.

---

[79] According to the 2012 Rape Crisis Center Survey conducted by the National Alliance to End Sexual Violence, 60 percent of victim advocates earn $20,000–$30,000 per year, http://endsexualviolence.org/where-we-stand/2012-rape-crisis-center-survey (accessed August 31, 2012).

[80] Grant Thornton, 2010, 2009 National Board Governance Survey for Not-for-Profit Organizations, (New York: Grant Thornton LLP).

cap on the Crime Victims Fund to ensure that forward progress in the victim assistance field is not checked.

Challenges

Too many victim service organizations struggle with staff recruitment and retention. They are mired in the daily demands of service provision, unable to direct human and financial capital to the building blocks of strategic planning, staff training and professional development, and program evaluation.

The field does not have a uniform, comprehensive benchmarking system for evaluating performance. Federal and state agencies have not established standardized performance measures that could be integrated into electronic case management systems to allow victim service providers to track performance with greater ease and effectiveness. Technology certainly offers a partial solution, yet too many programs lack the technology to streamline the collection and analysis of data to assess performance, and federal and state agencies have not taken concrete steps to work together to develop relevant and standardized performance measures for victim serving organizations.

A domestic violence shelter faced with the choice of turning away women and children in need of safety versus investing in program evaluation or staff training ultimately falters in its mission. It does not have to be this way. More programmatic and funding flexibility to invest in the infrastructure of the victim assistance field, can transform our field in the coming decades.

The National Victim Assistance Standards Consortium has brought disparate constituencies of the field together to assess and recommend standards for all victim service providers. Established in 1999 by OVC, in partnership with the University of South Carolina's Center for Child and Family Studies, the original consortium drafted a common definition and mission for the field of victim assistance, identified core individual and program standards, and disseminated these standards in 2003 to provide guidelines for promoting competence, ethical integrity, and quality and consistency of service. The consortium is now working to update the standards; *Achieving Excellence: Model Standards for Serving Victims & Survivors of Crime* will be available in 2013, along with supplemental materials for use in adapting the standards to meet individual or organizational needs.

CHAPTER 6
Making the "Vision" a Reality: Recommendations for Action

This Vision 21 report describes a watershed opportunity in the history of the victim assistance field. Although stakeholders recounted tremendous progress over the past three decades in securing victims' rights, protections, and services, the lack of qualitative and quantitative research on the experiences of crime victims in this country makes progress difficult to define. Despite advances, stakeholders were adamant that far more must be done to serve crime victims. They shared their concern, bolstered by available data, that many crime victims receive little or no assistance; and too many victim service organizations, especially programs serving victims of domestic violence, sexual assault, and child maltreatment, struggle to maintain the status quo—to provide even baseline services for victims. Stakeholders embraced the idea of transformational change, but warned that the lack of data, inadequate funding, and statutory restrictions pose formidable barriers.

The victim assistance field began as a movement for change that swept across this Nation; the passage of VOCA transformed advocacy into meaningful rights and services for crime victims. Now, as decades ago, we must continue to work with Congress to further the cause of crime victims. We believe the recommendations in this chapter can shape this important national dialogue.

Recommendations

1. Strategic planning at all levels should be continuous, not episodic.

Vision 21 is an important first step in facilitating an ongoing national conversation about the future of this field. Participants indicated that Vision 21 provided their only opportunity to engage with a broad spectrum of providers, advocates, and policymakers to address crime victim issues through a lens broader than their everyday work. Recognizing the need to continue engagement with the field and the complexity of implementing the recommendations outlined in this chapter, the strategic planning process initiated by Vision 21 should continue—at OVC and all levels of the field.

At the federal level, OVC should institutionalize an ongoing strategic planning process to fulfill its federal leadership mission, perhaps by establishing a working group comprising representatives from major crime victim constituencies to calibrate federal efforts with continuous feedback from the field and to analyze available data.

At the state and community levels, organizations and agencies should institutionalize a cross-cutting strategic planning process involving all stakeholders. Planning should focus on coordinated community responses and system linkages, program evaluation, and funding diversification to ensure a continuum of services for all crime victims. Strategic planning at the state level would maximize the impact of limited resources and eliminate duplicative funding efforts. State-level planning processes should include other state agencies; VOCA sub-recipients; state domestic violence, sexual assault, tribal, and other crime victim assistance coalitions; and victim assistance organizations integral to providing a continuum of services for crime victims.

2. End the research gap.

No comprehensive body of empirical data exists to guide policymakers, funders, and practitioners in the victims field, yet we know information is critical to victim-centered practice and policy. Expanding the body of knowledge about victimization is a collective responsibility to be embraced by all. At the federal level, OVC should partner with BJS and NIJ to shape the direction of crime victim-related research. Other federal and state agencies, including OVW, the Office of Juvenile Justice and Delinquency Prevention, relevant agencies from the U.S. Department of Health and Human Services, and major stakeholder constituency groups, including state VOCA administrators, should also participate and provide input. Together, these agencies should address gaps in basic research, evidence-based practices, and program evaluation as outlined in this report to develop a cohesive and strategic research agenda. Specific issues include the need to pursue the following:

▪ **Generate, collect, and analyze quantitative and qualitative data at the local and national levels on the incidence and prevalence of all forms of criminal victimization by—**

  · Expanding NCVS to capture richer data, including more detailed data on the pervasive crimes of domestic violence, sexual victimization, and child abuse, as well as new data on emerging types of victimization. The expansion should include more descriptive information about victims, the services they do or do not receive, and help-seeking behavior. This research will help identify the service gaps the field has shared anecdotally for years, but has never documented scientifically.

  · Expanding the use of the FBI's NIBRS to complete a nationally representative system of police administrative records describing crimes, victims, and police responses to victimization. This information will generate a greater understanding of specific types of victimization and subgroups of victims not currently captured by victim surveys. The data will also allow comparison between victims known to law enforcement with those served by victim service agencies to more readily identify underserved groups.

▪ **Develop a pragmatic and strategic approach to the development of evidence-based practices (EBPs) and program evaluation for victim-serving agencies and organizations.** Crime victim service providers should expand their use of practices that have been proved to be

effective and reliable for the broad array of victims they serve. These providers must also make ongoing evaluation an integral part of their programming to ensure continual quality control and improvement in support of victim safety and well-being. They must continually assess the effectiveness of practices now in use and new practices as they are developed. In addition, state VOCA administering agencies should explore ways to encourage funding applicants through incentives to use EBPs and program evaluation. The strategy should focus on providing additional funding, training, and technical assistance at the community level, not penalizing programs that lack the capacity to implement an empirical approach.

▪ **Develop federal agency-wide standardized performance measures.** Federal agencies should work together to develop standardized performance measures related to the provision of federally funded victim-related services and training and technical assistance. Ultimately, this would streamline the reporting burden on organizations receiving federal funding and provide more meaningful data for state and federal agencies, as well as Congress, to assess the overall impact of federally funded victim assistance. At the state and local levels, state administering agencies and sub-recipient organizations should commit to working with OVC, OVW, and other federal agencies to standardize performance measures related to victim services and related training and technical assistance. Standardized performance measures would serve as a critical first step toward streamlining and standardizing federal grant reporting.

▪ **Systematically study not just programs and practices but also the underlying infrastructure of victim-serving agencies and organizations in this country.** This assessment should look at factors such as reliance on volunteers, salaries and benefits of paid practitioners, access to evidence-based training and technical assistance, use of technology, sources of funding and subsequent administrative and reporting requirements, and demographic makeup of staff and leadership.

- **Evaluate the extent of enforcement of crime victims' rights and statutes at the tribal, state, and federal levels.** The evaluation should also address the impact and adequacy of professional legal representation on the broad array of crime victims' legal needs, including rights enforcement, immigration relief, and civil legal assistance.

- **Solve the research-to-practice gap.** Recognizing the need to bridge the long-standing and seemingly intractable translation gap between researchers and practitioners in the victim assistance field, federal agencies that administer victim-related grant funding must move beyond supportive language to take concrete action. They should work with Congress to find a solution, such as a third-party crime victim research and practice translation center, to institutionalize the communication necessary to translate research to practice and practice to research.

3. Build and institutionalize capacity.

Vision 21 stakeholders believe victim assistance in this country should be as universal as law enforcement response. Even in the face of prohibitive barriers, they outlined concrete first steps the victim assistance field can take to institutionalize access to rights and services for all crime victims in the United States. The building blocks of an innovative and results-oriented culture for the field include strategic planning; the use of technology to improve access to services and reduce administrative burdens; investments in human capital to recruit, train, and retain a diverse and professional workforce; and reliance on victimization data, EBPs, and program evaluation.

At the federal and state levels, OVC should establish an interagency working group to work with state VOCA administering agencies to—

- **Identify steps needed to develop a technology infrastructure** to increase the profile, accessibility, and responsiveness of victim-serving organizations and agencies and foster efficiencies and increased accountability.

- **Promote the systematic and innovative use of technology** to expand practitioner access to evidence-based training and technical assistance.

- **Promote and begin to institutionalize the application of EBPs and program evaluation in the victim assistance field.**

- **Foster adaptation of sustainability models that are used successfully in the nonprofit sector for victim assistance and advocacy organizations,** including the use of strategic planning, investments in human capital, and funding diversification.

Tribal, state, and national level victim organizations should formally link and leverage their largely separate advocacy efforts to develop unified and comprehensive policy and programming initiatives, address the intersection of prevention and victim services, raise national consciousness about victimization, and promote the critical system linkages that are needed in the 21st century to serve all victims of crime.

4. Partner with Congress to ensure flexibility and innovation in programming and funding.

During a time of financial constraint, when many victim assistance organizations struggle to maintain daily operations, stakeholders could have viewed Vision 21 as an intriguing but ultimately theoretical exercise. They could have dismissed the idea of extending victims' rights and services to support those who never report their victimization, as well as the crime victims who never receive services. Instead Vision 21 stakeholders were clear that timidity and resignation are not part of this field's vocabulary. They systematically outlined initial steps to promote progress, yet initial steps are just the beginning. Stakeholders believe it is time to work with Congress to provide the statutory and programmatic flexibility to meet the challenges of the 21st century. They outlined the following actions to catalyze needed change.

- **Recognizing the extremely complex funding formulation language in VOCA, OVC should join with state VOCA administrators and other key constituencies to work with Congress to address the following:**

  - Revision of the funding formula to expand assistance to more crime victims and strengthen the administrative framework to effectively manage funding. Although the majority of VOCA funding goes to states, the administering agencies may use only 5 percent of that funding to administer and monitor the funding at the sub-grantee level, as well as to support training, technical assistance, and program evaluation. For example, incremental raises of the Fund cap and increased administrative funding could be tied to state and OVC commitments to expand programmatic data collection, standardize performance measures, and integrate EBPs to the extent practicable.

- The implications of increasing the amount of formula funding for state and territorial crime victim compensation funds. Currently, VOCA funding is directly tied to the amount of state funding used to reimburse crime victims; consequently, increases or decreases in the annual cap on the Fund impact only the formula victim assistance funding going to the states, not formula victim compensation funding. Substantive variations in the types of expenses covered and crime victim eligibility among the states and territories could also be addressed.

- The advisability of revising statutory language to address emerging issues. VOCA's statutory framework sometimes hinders the use of funding to solve myriad policy and programmatic issues. It is largely silent on the value of research and program evaluation, the use of technology, the need for collaborative and frequently multijurisdictional responses to victims, support of services at the national and international levels, and the capacity of organizations to address what we now understand are the complex and longer-term needs of crime victims.

- **Recognizing that new challenges call for new solutions, it is worth revisiting the authorizations for VOCA-funded programs to address their reach, efficacy, and accountability.** Innovation has always been the hallmark of the victim assistance field; improving and better aligning funding to improve research, capacity building, and

accountability would promote exponential progress. Stakeholders called for attention to the following:

- Support of critical victim-related research by BJS and NIJ to initiate and continue foundational work to address the research gaps identified in this report.

- Support for improved assistance to victims, including information, referrals, and online and hotline services. At the national level, the goal would be to assist victims who do not receive assistance from existing state programs. There is currently no authorizing language in VOCA allowing OVC to support operational expenses of organizations that could provide these services, similar to community-level organizations.

- Support for building capacity and infrastructure at the state and local levels. More flexible assistance might be allocated to states, over the course of several years, to target statewide needs assessments and strategic planning, an expanded use of technology, comprehensive program evaluation, and the provision of evidence-based training and technical assistance. States might be permitted to use funding to develop and evaluate demonstration projects to reach and serve more victims and to build the capacity of organizations that have not been able to access VOCA funding.

- Support of holistic legal assistance for crime victims. Funding could build on the promise of the Crime Victims' Rights Act of 2004 and other landmark federal legislation, such as VAWA and the Trafficking Victims Protection Act, to transform the legal landscape for crime victims. Stakeholders spoke of a national network of wraparound legal assistance to address not only the enforcement of crime victims' rights, but also the wider range of victims' needs, such as assistance with identity theft and other forms of financial fraud and civil legal assistance. These networks would provide the linkages between existing pockets of available legal services and fill critical gaps on a statewide and perhaps regional basis.

- Support for American Indian and Alaska Native victims. Stakeholders recognized the need to target resources for federally recognized tribes, tribal organizations, and federal agencies responsible for victim assistance in Indian Country. OVC and the victim assistance field, particularly tribal advocacy organizations, should work with Congress to ensure that victims in Indian Country are no longer a footnote to this country's response to crime victims.

- Successfully positioning the victim assistance field in the 21st century is the responsibility of many. The Vision 21 initiative was a labor of resolve, intense examination, passion, and courage to transcend conventional boundaries to focus on a goal grander than our everyday work. We stand ready to work with one another and Congress to fulfill the promise of Vision 21: Transforming Victim Services.

References

American Academy of Child and Adolescent Psychiatry. 1998. "Practice Parameters for the Assessment and Treatment of Children with Posttraumatic Stress Disorder." *Journal of the American Academy of Child and Adolescent Psychiatry,* 37(10 Supplement):,4S–26S.

Cohen, J.A., Berliner, L. & March, J.S. 2000. "Treatment of Children and Adolescents." In E.B. Foa, T.M. Keane, M.J. Friedman, & J.A. Cohen (Eds.), *Effective Treatments for PTSD: Practice Guidelines from the International Society for Traumatic Stress Studies.* New York: The Guilford Press, 106–138.

Cohen, J.A., Mannarino, A.P. & Deblinger, E. 2006. *Treating Trauma and Traumatic Grief in Children and Adolescents.* New York: The Guilford Press.

Gould, S.J. 1981. *The Mismeasure of Man.* W.W. Norton & Company Inc.: New York & London.

Prinz, R.J., Sanders, M.R., Shapiro, C.J., Whitaker, D.J. & Lutzker, J.R. 2009. "Population-Based Prevention of Child Maltreatment: The U.S. Triple P System Population Trial." *Prevention Science* 10(1) (March 2009): 1–12

Acknowledgments

OVC gratefully acknowledges the many individuals and organizations who contributed to this initiative and the preparation of the final report. Without their assistance, the contents of this report would not represent the insights, opinions, experiences, values, and vision of the victim assistance field.

Most especially, we express gratitude to the report's major contributors. These individuals include Vision 21 project directors and senior staff, writers, editors, and OVC staff:

Angela Begle, Ph.D., Medical University of South Carolina

Joy Davis, Office for Victims of Crime (Contractor)

Jack Fleming, formerly National Center for Victims of Crime

Joye E. Frost, Office for Victims of Crime

Meg Garvin, National Crime Victim Law Institute

Charity Hope, Vera Institute of Justice

Susan Howley, National Center for Victims of Crime

Dean Kilpatrick, Ph.D., Medical University of South Carolina

Julie Landrum, formerly National Crime Victim Law Institute

Meg Morrow, Office for Victims of Crime

Kevin O'Brien, Ed.D., formerly National Center for Victims of Crime

William H. Petty, Ph.D., Office for Victims of Crime (Fellow)

Mary Rappaport (Consultant)

Benjamin Saunders, Ph.D., Medical University of South Carolina

Jennifer Shewmake, Office for Victims of Crime Training and Technical Assistance Center

Nancy Smith, Vera Institute of Justice

Cheryl Tyiska, Office for Victims of Crime Training and Technical Assistance Center

We also wish to acknowledge the many people who supported the critical components of the initiative, including stakeholder forum participants, subject matter experts, OVC staff, and numerous other individuals from the field—all of whom provided invaluable expertise, insight, input, and feedback. For their commitment and diligence, we gratefully acknowledge the following:

The Role of the Crime Victims Field in the U.S. Response to Crime and Delinquency Stakeholder Forum Attendees (Participant List)

Emerging Challenges in the Crime Victims Field Stakeholder Forum Attendees (Participant List)

Enduring Challenges in the Crime Victims Field Stakeholder Forum Attendees (Participant List)

Building Capacity in the Crime Victims Field Stakeholder Forum Attendees (Participant List)

Project Synthesis Stakeholder Forum Attendees (Participant List)

Thomas Abt, Office of Justice Programs

Jacqueline Agtuca, Sacred Circle, National Congress of American Indians Task Force on Violence Against Native Women

Kira Antell, U.S. Sentencing Commission

Michael de Arellano, Ph.D., Medical University of South Carolina

Mary Atlas-Terry, Office for Victims of Crime

Bethany Backes, National Institute of Justice

Emily Bauernfeind, Office for Victims of Crime (Contractor)

Lisa Brunner, White Earth Nation

Bethany Case, Office for Victims of Crime (Fellow)

Jasmine D'Addario-Fobian, Office for Victims of Crime

Steve Derene, National Association of VOCA Assistance Administrators

Janice Delaney, Office of Communications, Office of Justice Programs (Contractor)

Juana Majel Dixon, National Congress of American Indians and Pauma Band of Luiseño Indians

Rebecca Dreke, National Center for Victims of Crime

Dan Eddy, National Association of Crime Victim Compensation Boards

Kathleen Gless, Office for Victims of Crime

Whitney Grubbs (Consultant)

Josy Hahn, Vera Institute of Justice

Susan Herman, Department of Criminal Justice, Pace University

Lenora (Lynn) Hootch, Yupik Eskimo

JoAnn Horn, Emmonak Women's Shelter

Laura Ivkovich, Office for Victims of Crime

Shadine Jankovic, Office for Victims of Crime

Paula Julian, La Jolla Band of Luiseño Indians

Lynn Langton, Ph.D., Bureau of Justice Statistics

John Laub, Ph.D., National Institute of Justice

Mary Lou Leary, Office of Justice Programs

James Lynch, Ph.D., Bureau of Justice Statistics

Jaimee Napp, formerly Office for Victims of Crime (Fellow)

William Sabol, Ph.D., Bureau of Justice Statistics

Lindy Schlater, La Jolla Band of Luiseño Indians

Wendy Schlater, La Jolla Band of Luiseño Indians

Steve Siegel, Denver District Attorney's Office

Lucy Simpson, National Indigenous Women's Resource Center

Tyson Simpson, Clan Star

Gloria Tate, formerly Vera Institute of Justice

Debra Whitcomb, Office for Victims of Crime (Fellow)

The final report also benefited from the input of numerous VOCA administrators who participated in meetings and conference workshops devoted to discussions of Vision 21, as well as informal feedback from VOCA administrators as the initiative progressed. Finally, a work of this magnitude cannot include the names of every person who contributed in some way. For all others whose names do not appear here, but without whose assistance Vision 21 would not have drawn to a successful conclusion, we also offer our deepest appreciation. Most of all, we thank the many victims/survivors and victim service providers throughout the country from whom we learn every day.

Appendix

The first places to look for answers are the two major national crime data research programs that measure the magnitude, nature, and, to a more limited degree, the impact of crime in the United States. The U.S. Department of Justice (DOJ) administers both of these programs: the Federal Bureau of Investigation's **Uniform Crime Reports (UCR)** and the Bureau of Justice Statistics' **National Crime Victimization Survey (NCVS)**.

UCR is an annual compilation of offense and arrest data reported voluntarily by more than 17,000 local police departments nationwide. UCR data reflect only the most serious offenses associated with each criminal incident; it includes two types of offenses, Part I and II, but reports only those Part II offenses for which an arrest has been made.[1] Except in its Supplementary Homicide Reports, UCR does not measure the impact of crime on victims.

NCVS is a continuous telephone and in-person survey of a nationally representative sample of about 147,000 persons age 12 or older from 82,000 households.[2] It provides data on personal crime victimizations: rape and sexual assault, robbery, aggravated or simple assault, and larceny and household property crime, including burglary, motor vehicle, and other types of theft. NCVS encompasses data on crimes reported and not reported to police, as well as limited data on the type of assistance provided by law enforcement (when the crimes are reported) and whether the victim received services from a victim service agency.

Separate NCVS supplements also provide statistics on stalking, identity theft (which includes the misuse of a victim's existing accounts or personal information to engage in fraudulent activity), school crime, and contacts between the police and the public. NCVS does not cover such crimes as homicide, fraud, vandalism, and arson; crimes against children under 12; or crimes against businesses or other institutions.

Some crimes, such as alcohol- and drug-related traffic incidents, are not tracked by either UCR or NCVS (although UCR does report on arrests of persons for driving while intoxicated), but data on these are available from other federal sources, such as the National Highway Traffic Safety Administration. While NCVS statistics are generated at the national level, BJS is also developing ways to produce state and local estimates of victimization.

Users seeking complete victim information that includes racial categories and gender identity will not have an easy time. UCR does not provide data on victim characteristics for any crimes except for homicide. The FBI's National Incident-Based Reporting System (NIBRS), begun in the early 1990s, includes detailed information on crimes and victims, but NIBRS data cover only 28 percent of the resident population in the United States.

UCR reports both on the number of hate and bias crimes and on the nature of the bias against victims based on their sexual orientation. For UCR reporting purposes, bias is reported only if investigation of an incident reveals sufficient information to lead a prudent person to conclude that the offender's actions were motivated in whole or part by bias. UCR provides data on several categories of victims' sexual orientation (for example, lesbian, gay, and bisexual).

---

[1] Part I offenses include homicide, rape, robbery, aggravated assault, burglary, larceny, theft, motor vehicle theft, and arson. Part II offenses include a variety of other offenses, including simple assault. Only in the arrest statistics does the UCR track the race of offenders (arrestees); however, it does not track their ethnicity and places persons of Hispanic or Latino origin in one of four racial categories; white (including Latino), black, American Indian/Alaska Native, and Pacific Islander. For more information, see www.fbi.gov/about-us/cjis/ucr/ucr.

[2] Once selected, households remain in the sample for 3 years and eligible persons in these households are interviewed every 6 months, for a total of seven interviews. New households rotate into the sample to replace households whose 3 years are up. The sample includes persons living in group quarters, such as dormitories, rooming houses, and religious group dwellings, but excludes persons living in military barracks and institutional settings, such as correctional or hospital facilities, and the homeless. For more information, see the *Survey Methodology for Criminal Victimization in the United States, 2007*, NCJ 227669, March 2010, on the BJS Web site at www.bjs.gov.

NCVS obtains data for persons of single and multiracial categories and obtains information on the Hispanic or Latino origin of persons separately from their race.[3] Because of differences in methodology, crime coverage, and crime definitions, the data and trends tracked by NIBRS, UCR, and NCVS cannot be easily compared, which contributes to confusion for practitioners and others seeking a clear overview of crime victimization in the United States.

---

[3] For more information, see http://bjs.ojp.usdoj.gov/index.cfm?ty=dcdetail&iid=245.